Crossing the 'river of fire' : the socialism of William Morris

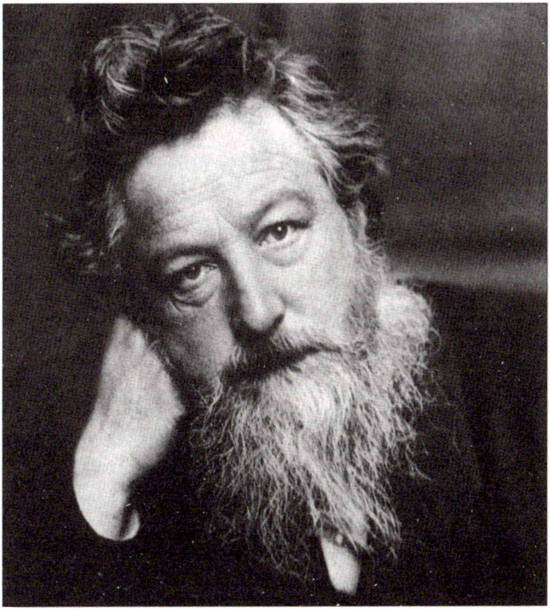

REVOLUTIONARY PORTRAIT: 8

Crossing the river of fire: the socialism of William Morris
by Hassan Mahamdallie
Published June 2008
by REDWORDS
1 Bloomsbury Street, London WC1B 3QE
www.redwords.org.uk

Second edition with minor corrections *2013*

ISBN: 978 1 909026 04 9

Design and production: Roger Huddle
Set in Monotype Janson, Franklin Gothic & Franklin Gothic Condensed
Printed by Halstan Printing Ltd.

© Hassan Mahamdallie

Redwords is linked to Bookmarks the Socialist Bookshop
www.bookmarksbookshop.co.uk

REDWORDS

Crossing the 'river of fire' : the socialism of William Morris

by Hassan Mahamdallie

About the author:

Hassan Mahamdallie has written and lectured widely on race in contemporary Britain and on Black history. Trained in theatre, he has made a living as an actor, director, writer, arts-in-education worker, anti-racist activist and journalist. Recent articles include, Muslim working class struggles in Britain, and a contribution to a collection of writings *Tell It Like It Is: How Our Schools Fail Black Chidren*. Hassan presently works at Arts Council England where he has been responsible for developing a project on the relationship between artistic practise and the Islamic faith.

Dedication:

for Ayaan-Waad mahad santahey

Part 1	1	
		Notes 31
Part 2	35	
		Notes 61
Part 3	65	
		Notes 105

Bibliorahpy & further reading
111

William Morris:
    Chants for Socialists
        117

British colonial conquerer Cecil Rhodes stands astride Africa in 1892 cartoon from British magazine Punch

William Morris

— on War & Imperialism:

If war really becomes imminent our
duties as socialists are clear enough,
and do not differ from those we have
to act on ordinarily... that the interests
of the workmen are the same in all
countries and they can never really
be the enemies of each other; that
the men of our labouring classes,
therefore, should turn a deaf ear to the
recruiting sergeant, and refuse to allow
themselves be dressed up in red and be
taught to form a part of the modern
killing machine for the honour and
glory of a country in which they have
only a dog's share of many kicks and a
few halfpence.[1]

All wars now waged, under whatever
pretences, are really wars for the great
prizes in the world market.[2]

William Morris

— on Capitalism & the Environment:

It is profit which draws men into enormous unmanageable aggregations called towns, for instance; profit which crowds them up when they are there into quarters without gardens or open spaces; profit which won't take the most ordinary precautions against wrapping a whole district in a cloud of sulphurous smoke; which turns beautiful rivers into filthy sewers, which condemns all but the rich to live in houses idiotically cramped and confined at the best, and at the worst in houses for whose wretchedness there is no name.[3]

The Capitalist vampire from Justice *1885 by Walter Crane*

William Morris

— ON SWEATSHOP LABOUR:

The misery of those who are sweated, whether by the drill of factory or the many links of the sweated chain, is the high price to pay for the glory of sustaining a class of idle, rich men. Is the gain worth the price? [4]

— ON THE PROFIT SYSTEM:

That system, which I have called competitive commerce, is distinctly a system of war; that is of waste and destruction… the point of it being that under it whatever a man gains he gains at the expense of some other man's loss. Such a system cannot heed whether those who make them are degraded by their work: it heeds one thing and only one, namely, what is called making a profit…the plunder of the weak by the strong. [5]

Part 1

*A*GAINST WAR and imperialism, against the destruction of our environment, against exploitation and disaster capitalism, for humanity everywhere—set aside the old fashioned language for a moment. Do these words not speak to us about our world today?

Yet the above heart-felt convictions come to us, not from the present, but from the 19th century, delivered by a late-middle-aged middle-class Englishman, who, before he threw himself into the progressive movement of his time, was regarded as a member of the establishment whose previous claim to fame was writing epic poems indulged in by the Victorian middle classes![6]

Such is the remarkable person that was William Morris – a figure from history, yet whose fiery arguments seem to chime absolutely with our present times. But if he is known at all today it is for his contribution as a designer and artist. We certainly shouldn't dismiss Morris's achievements in this field; his furnishings and textile work, his ever popular wallpapers, carpets and 'Morris' chair, all still retain their balance of utility and beauty.

However, alongside these achievements rank his political writings, both fiction and non-fiction. These have influenced generations of working class activists. The talks he delivered to audiences across Britain propelled those who caught them into their own struggles against exploitation, injustice and inequality. His radical prose works, especially *The Dream of John Ball*, *The Pilgrims of Hope* and the ever popular *News From Nowhere*, were regarded as influential enough to be translated into many different languages. In the 1930s the Labour Party intellectual Harold Laski found copies of Morris's books in the houses of impoverished miners in the north east of England when their furniture had long since been sold. Morris's writings on environmentalism broke new ground, identifying catastrophic trends in the way capitalism was already putting the planet at peril and arguing for measures that the world's politicians still shrink from. Morris was extraordinarily prolific. No wonder a doctor put down his cause of death as 'Simply being William Morris, and having done more work than most ten men'. Ironically it is the very diversity of his work that has allowed the type of people Morris fought tooth and nail in his lifetime to claim his legacy today.

Morris's writings apparently taught 1960s Labour minister Barbara Castle 'that socialism was not merely about struggle, but sensual fulfilment, and it gave her hope'. But Morris sided with the working class far more consistently than Labour governments have done. Today's Labour ministers' default position is to condemn strikes and back the employers, irrespective of the merits of the workers' case. In 1888, backing the match girls' strike in east London, Morris wrote, 'If there were no strikes...the manufacturing capitalists would have an easy time of it, and would reduce the workers under their control to the very lowest point of misery'.[7] Morris would have given short shrift to the Barbara Castle's draconian *In Place of Strife* measures — her 1969 Labour government anti trade union proposals, which planned to lock up strikers who took unofficial action.

Tony Blair is a fan of Morris's political writings. They were an inspiration when he was at Oxford University, we have been told. However, it is unlikely that Blair would agree with Morris's description of parliament in *News From Nowhere* as a 'dung market'. Would Blair agree with Morris's analysis that 'to avoid the disaster of gaining the doubtful alliance of the well-to-do at the expense of losing the support of the poor, it is surely necessary to never cease saying: The test of the realisation of socialism will be the abolition of property'.[8] It's also unlikely that Gordon Brown will ever greet the demise of a monarch with the pithy comment 'Dead at last', as did Morris on the death of tyrant Frederick III of Germany.

The hundredth anniversary of Morris's death in 1996 provoked extraordinary abuse. 'He was not just a wallpaper designer, but a revolutionary socialist, a combination that might have been the invention of a satirist', wrote one critic. Another declared, 'His politics are not only irrelevant but objectionable'. One made the ridiculous and hysterical claim that 'Morris can be seen as an inspiration...for the Khmer Rouge... He was no totalitarian, but in the Phnom Penh of Year Zero, there is a hideous echo of *News From Nowhere*'.[9]

The legacy of William Morris deserves much, much more than to be locked in a false embrace by unprincipled and

WHEN ADAM DELVED AND EVE SPAN,
WHO WAS THEN THE GENTLEMAN?

Edward Burne-Jones illustration as frontispiece for A Dream of John Ball

CROSSING THE RIVER OF FIRE:

unscrupulous politicians or derided by ignorant newspaper hacks. His achievements certainly deserve to be rediscovered by a new generation of artists, activists and socialists, because if you could sum up Morris's message to the Victorian working class it would surely be 'Another world is possible'. We should look at him not so much as an interesting historical figure, but as a contemporary voice and an inspiration to all those today who strive for radical change. For William Morris the artist was also William Morris the revolutionary socialist. In 1884 at the age of 49 he set himself against the establishment and crossed what he described as the 'river of fire'. He joined the 200 or so Marxist revolutionaries in Britain at that time, and worked unceasingly until his death in 1896 for the cause of socialism. Morris wrote the declaration for the Socialist League, the revolutionary party he founded in 1885. It began, 'Fellow citizens, we come before you as a body advocating the principles of revolutionary international socialism; that is, we seek a change in the basis of society — a change which would destroy the distinctions of classes and nationalities'.[10]

MORRIS HAS often been caricatured as a dreamer, a utopian who had little to say about how this new society was to come about. However, dreams of utopia have rarely been worthless – they have always been about projecting a better future onto a dark and seemingly unchanging present. Morris's great achievement was to struggle to close that gap between what is and what might be. Central to his understanding of socialism was also the cast iron belief in revolutionary organisation as a vehicle for fundamental change. That was always the centre of his activity from his wide ranging newspaper articles, pamphlets and books to his lectures and campaigns. And apart from a short period in the 1890s Morris's political career was always bound up with a revolutionary organisation — first the Social Democratic Federation and then the Socialist League.

At the centre of Morris's politics was also the belief that profound change in society was reliant on the self-activity of working people. Many of us can agree that change is needed – but what force will bring it about? You have to combine and unify to force change. In one of his many lectures Morris told the Staffordshire School of Art, 'When the day comes that there is a serious strike of workmen against the poisoning of the air with smoke or the waters with filth, I shall think that art is getting on indeed'.[11]

Also important to an understanding of Morris is his belief in fundamental change. He was a standard bearer of social revolution in Victorian Britain, not an easy flag to fly by any measure. In 1887, defending the Paris Commune of 1871, which came about when for a short time that city was controled by the working class, he wrote:

> The revolution itself will raise those for whom the revolution must be made. Their newborn hope translated into action will develop their human and social qualities, and the new struggle itself will fit them to receive the benefits of the new life which revolution will make possible for them. It is for boldly seizing the opportunity offered for thus elevating the mass of the workers into heroism that we now celebrate the men of the Paris Commune.[12]

Even the great social historian E P Thompson, in his pathbreaking biography of Morris, written in 1956, and intended to save Morris from reaction and keep the revolutionary spirit alive in the midst of Stalinism and the Cold War, tends to play down the insurrectionary stance Morris took. Less distinguished biographers have tried to separate Morris the artist from Morris the socialist. For some, this meant isolating his art from his politics. For others, it meant ignoring his artistic output altogether. In reality, the two were indissolubly linked. What is fascinating about Morris's art is that it expressed precisely the conditions and contradictions of the period and in it one can trace the trajectory of his political career.

William Morris was born in 1834 in Walthamstow, north London, into a wealthy middle class family, immersed 'in the ordinary bourgeois style of comfort'. His birthplace was at that time 'a suburban village on the edge of the Epping Forest, and once a pleasant place enough, but now terribly cockneyfied and choked-up by the jerry built". [13] His father had moved to London from Worcester in the 1820s to join a firm of City stockbrokers. When William was ten his father acquired 272 £1 shares in a new Devonshire copper mining company. Within six months the shares, due to the discovery that the mines were richer than at first believed, were worth £200,000, a fortune for those times. Of course, one consequence was that William and the rest of the family didn't have to worry about money. But Morris's father's 'good fortune' is also an indication of the economic and political changes that were being wrought in society.

While the young William was growing up, British society was changing rapidly. The watershed politically was 1848 – the year the British working class in the form of the Chartists suffered a historic defeat at the hands of a fast maturing British state. The Chartists were the first mass workers movement. They agitated and fought for a 'People's Charter' of universal suffrage, no property qualifications for voters, annual parliaments, workers pay for MPs and vote by the ballot box. Their demands threw down a fundamental challenge to the (corrupt) order of things, but the ruling class at the end of the day faced down the Chartists, proving itself to be more ruthless than its democratic opponents. The period that followed was marked by what historian John Saville has persuasively defined as 'the consolidation of the capitalist state'.[14]

This enforced political stability brought British capitalism a period of continuous economic expansion between 1848 and 1874, shaping the world which Morris was to grow up in. This meant that:

> For some 30 years British capital was in the happy position of enjoying a world in which an expanding market and ever-increasing profits seemed to be a law of nature, in which even the least efficient manufacturer could prosper and the more pushing and resolute prospered fabulously.[15]

This expansion sucked labour into the cities, creating rapid unplanned urbanisation and industrialisation. The slums and smokestacks, that were a mark of Victorian prosperity, were also a symbol of, as Morris himself put it, 'all the incredible filth, disorder and degradation of modern civilisation'.

The worst aspects of these slums were dealt with, beginning in the 1840s, after repeated epidemics of cholera, typhus and smallpox demonstrated to the ruling class that certain reforms in sanitation and sewerage systems were desirable from their point of view. However, that did not mean that the working class of the cities were lifted in some philanthropic way out of the degradation imposed on them. It was rather that, as Frederick Engels put it in 1892, 'the bourgeoisie have made further progress in the art of hiding the distress of the working class' and as Morris was later to write, 'Under present conditions, almost the whole labour imposed by civilisation on the "lower classes" is unwholesome; that is to say that people's lives are shortened by it; and yet because we don't see people's throats cut before our eyes we think nothing of it'. [16]

But what the prosperity of British capitalism did mean was that it was possible to believe you could take steps to improve your life. Some people blocked from advancement at home emigrated in search of a decent life. It has been estimated that between 1852 and 1868 some 3 million people emigrated mainly to America and 'the Dominions' such as Canada and Australia. The fictional representatives of this new phenomenon of mass economic migration were the Micawber family in Charles Dickens's *David Copperfield* published in 1850 (Dickens was a favourite of Morris's). As Mrs Micawber says on the eve of their voyage to the New World:

> From the first moment of this voyage, I wish Mr Micawber to stand upon that vessel's prow and say, 'Enough of delay, enough of disappointment, enough of limited means.

That was the old country. This is the new. Produce your reparation. Bring it forward!

The other side was the general improvement in the lives of a narrow grouping of skilled workers who banded together in the belief that if they exerted sufficient pressure on the employers they could wrest improvements in wages and conditions from them within the framework of capitalism. Thus it was that powerful 'New Model Unions' were formed. The Amalgamated Society of Engineers (ASE) was the most prominent, founded in 1851. It was a national craft union: only those who had gone through the appropriate apprenticeship could join its ranks. It was highly centralised, with a rigid set of rules that controlled what local branches could do — they couldn't call strikes unless they had the authority of national officials. All sorts of benefits were open to members — sick benefits, unemployment benefits, even emigration payments. These took precedence over strikes. So between 1851 and 1889 the ASE paid out £2,987,993 on benefits compared to £87,613 for strikes.

The view of the leaders of the New Model Unions like the ASE was that labour was a commodity and exploitation a fact of life — their role was to try and up the bargaining power of their members by regulating the supply of labour to the bosses. This was exemplified by a saying of the time:

Lads unite to better your condition:
When eggs are scarce, eggs are dear;
When men are scarce, men are dear.[17]

That is not to say that unions like the ASE never struck, but they were confined to a layer of skilled workers and were expressly limited to economic aims, at least on the part of the leadership. It would be also be a mistake to believe that the class struggle had died away completely. For instance, in 1853 the remnants of the Chartist movement mobilised national support for striking Preston weavers. In 1855 some 200,000 people gathered in Hyde Park to oppose a government bill prohibiting Sunday trading (Sunday being the only day workers had time to enjoy leisure).

In the 1860s there was significant support among English workers for the northern states in the American Civil War; being against slavery and the South, whereas the English upper classes were desperate to come to the aid of the slave-owners. Lancashire cotton workers resisted taking the side of the South, despite the fact that a blockade on slave-picked cotton plunged them into desperate hardship. Anti-slavery agitators from North America such as the inspirational black leader Fredrick Douglass toured Britain, drawing in huge and sympathetic crowds. This reception in turn had a profound effect on Douglass, convincing him that racism was a social construct, not an inevitability. In Britain Douglass found his 'self' transformed:

> I breathe, and lo! The chattel becomes a man! I gaze around in vain for one who will question my equal humanity, claim me as a slave, or offer me an insult. I employ a cab — I am seated beside white people — I am shown into the same parlour — I dine at the same table — and no one is offended. No delicate nose grows deformed in my presence. I find no difficulty here in obtaining admission into any place of worship, instruction, or amusement, on equal terms with people as white as any I ever saw in the United States. I meet nothing to

remind me of my complexion. I find myself regarded and treated at every turn with kindness and deference paid to white people. When I go to church I am met by no upturned nose and scornful lip, to tell me — 'We don't allow niggers in here'.[18]

In contrast pro-slavery speakers found themselves literally run out of town and city. This anti-racist stance was one of the finest acts of solidarity the British working class has ever shown. (Indeed it was this mass demonstration of principle that encouraged Marx and Engels in 1864 to set up a transcontinental network of socialists known as the First International.) In 1866 the defeat of the Reform Bill to extend the voting franchise led to huge meetings across the country. Another 200,000-strong demonstration marched to Hyde Park and ignoring a banning order, tore down the railings in order to enter the park and meet. This pressure led to the 1867 Reform Act that, though far short of popular demands, succeeded in securing the vote for men of the lower middle classes and the better off sections of workers.

But for all this, there was a general absence of an independent, determined and organised working class outlook that had previously been shaped by the Chartists and their leaders. This led to an orientation and dependence on the Liberal Party and the formation of the Radical Clubs, which organised working class support for the Liberals. Even though the Radical leaders tended to be middle class, the composition of Radical Clubs was mainly working class. The leaders of the New Model Unions formed themselves into a 'junta' and pursued a cosy policy of class collaboration – taking their place at the left elbow of the Liberal Party.[19]

William Morris was later to learn that the Liberal Party would never be a vehicle for working class interests. As he wrote:

> On the fall of Chartists, the Liberal Party, a nondescript and flaccid creation of bourgeoisie supremacy, a party without principles or definition, but a thoroughly adequate expression of English middle class hypocrisy, cowardice, and short-sightedness, engrossed the whole of the political progressive movement in England, and dragged the working class along with it, blind as they were to their own interests and the solidarity of labour.[20]

This then was the social, economic and political world that faced Morris, and it seemed as if there was no escape. With no contact with the socialist flame being kept flickering in London by Karl Marx, Engels, a handful of émigrés, political refugees and ageing Chartists, there seemed to be no future but capitalism triumphant. There seemed to be no alternative but to retreat, harking back to the days before industrialism had ripped the landscape apart and inserted the profit motive into every aspect of human relations.

It is worth quoting at length Morris's description of this feeling of hopelessness and suffocation in his 1894 article *How I Became a Socialist*:

> The immediate future seemed to me likely to intensify all the present evils by sweeping away the last survivals of the days before the dull squalor of civilisation had settled down on the world. This was a bad outlook indeed, and if I may mention myself as a personality and not as a mere type, especially so to a man of my disposition, careless of metaphysics and religion, as well as of scientific analysis,

but with a deep love of the earth and the life on it, and a passion for the history of the past of mankind.

Think of it! Was it all to end in a counting house on the top of a cinder-heap, with Podsnap's drawing room in the offing and a Whig committee dealing out champagne to the rich and margarine to the poor in such convenient proportions as would make all men contented together? ... Yet believe me, in my heart, when I really forced myself to look towards the future, that is what I saw in it, and, as far as I could tell, scarce anyone seemed to think it worthwhile to struggle against such a consummation of civilisation.[21]

When Morris went up to Oxford in 1853 at the age of 21, the era of capitalist expansion looked as if it would stretch on forever. He soon fell into a circle of friends who set up a 'brotherhood' – a mock monastic order for a 'crusade and holy warfare against the age and the heartless coldness of the times'. Morris dallied briefly with Roman Catholicism at this time.

At the core of the brotherhood were Dante Gabriel Rossetti, Edward Burne-Jones, Ford Madox Brown and Morris's future wife and lifelong inspiration Jane Burden. They remained close companions and collaborators for the rest of Morris's life. Rossetti was to become the pre-eminent Pre-Raphaelite painter. He embodied a reform school in fine art that simultaneously looked back to mediaeval 'purity' and away from the ornate decorative styles of the day towards more realistic depictions of nature and people. The Pre-Raphaelites can be seen in this way as the fore-runners of the modernist movement of the 20th century. The artist and designer Burne-Jones, along with fellow artist Ford Madox Brown later joined with Morris in the founding of the London design company known as 'The Firm'.

Just as significant were the literary influences Morris was busily absorbing. He read the works of Thomas Carlyle, John Keats and John Ruskin. The influences of these three were to shape the rebellious young Morris and lay the foundations for his later political development.

Carlyle's *Past and Present*, published in 1843, was a 'blistering Old Testament attack on the morality of industrial capitalism, contrasted with an idealised picture of life in the monastery of St Edmunsbury in the 12th century'.[22] This obsession with the Middle Ages, which was portrayed as a time of honour, simplicity and morals, appealed to Morris and was to have a huge impact on his future artistic output.

The poet Keats was a contemporary and friend of Shelley and was radical in his sympathies and his actions. Keats's reaction to the unbearable nature of the society around him was to intensify the craftsmanship of the art he produced, through 'poetic' vocabulary and setting his poems in a dream or past times, whereby reality and the imagination merged. In a letter to Benjamin Bailey, Keats reflected, 'the thought that we are mortal makes us groan'.[23] Keats political leanings were heavily buried in his poetic style, as in Ode on a Grecian Urn:

When old age shall this generation waste,
    Thou shalt remain, in midst of other woe
Than ours, a friend to man, to whom thou say'st,
    'Beauty is truth, truth beauty, — that is all
Ye know on earth, and all ye need to know.'

For Morris this approach provided a model of escape. As he wrote in 1885, 'We were born into a dull time oppressed with bourgeoisdom and philistinism so sorely that we were forced to turn back on ourselves, and only in ourselves and the world of art and literature was there any hope'.[24]

Above all the influence of John Ruskin is the key to understanding Morris's development. Ruskin was Morris's 'master'. In *How I Became A Socialist* Morris says, 'It was through him [Ruskin] that I learnt to give form to my discontent.' Ruskin in his work *The Nature of Gothic* (which Morris later published) compared medieval society to that of 19th century capitalism through architecture. Ruskin was no socialist, and was not even sympathetic to the working class as a class, but his great insight was to reject scornfully the curse of the modern age that reduced everything to its 'cash-nexus'. Everything and everybody had its price: 'Cash-payment never was, or could expect for a few years to be, the union-bond of man to man. Cash never yet paid one man fully his deserts to another; nor could it, nor can it, now or henceforth to the end of the world'.[25] Ruskin denounced the transformation of production away from the hands of craft workers — the mode of production of the middle ages — towards the modern factory system, the capitalist mode of production. The former was a 'human' mode of production, the latter 'inhuman':

> You must either make a tool of the creature, or a man of him. You cannot make both. Men were not intended to work with the accuracy of tools, to be precise and perfect in all their actions. If you will have that precision out of them, and make their fingers measure degrees like cog-

wheels, and their arms strike curves like compasses, you must unhumanise them.[26]

Morris embraced this view: if there was no way that society could go forward unless it was merely an intensification of the miseries that the factory system created, then to advocate the ways of the past was the only civilised thing to do. What attracted Morris to this argument was that in medieval times production was based on the handiwork of individuals; there was no separation between the workers and the 'fruit of their labour'. The craft workers gathered the raw materials, fashioned the entire product themselves, and then used it or sold it on.[27]

For Ruskin and his disciple the young Morris the replacement of this with 'filth, disorder and degradation' was unforgivable. In a significant way, of course, they were correct in their condemnation of capitalism. The machine had taken away livelihoods and replaced them with exploitation and alienation. As Morris put it, 'The system of a man working for himself leisurely and happily was infinitely better, both as regards the worker and his work, than that division of labour system which the profit-grinding of rising commercialism supplanted it by'.[28]

However, there was an essential element missing from both Ruskin and Morris's argument. Of course it was true that capitalism worked 'blindly, violently, destructively', but it had also increased the productive forces in society and with it the promise of meeting human need on a global scale for the first time in human history. Crucially, capitalism had transformed small producers into proletarians, and so had created the force that could, by revolution, lay hold of the means of production for the common good, putting an end to alienation and drudgery. As Engels had argued, the productive forces could thus be transformed from:

> Demoniacal masters into willing servants in the hands of the producers working in association. It is the difference between the destructive forces of electricity in the lightning of the thunderstorm and the tamed electricity of the telegraph and the arc light, the difference between a conflagration and a fire working in the services of man.[29]

After he had become a socialist Morris synthesised his early views, coined by E P Thompson as 'romanticism in revolt' with a deeper understanding of capitalism and its contradictions. So in 1884 he wrote:

> Of course it is impossible to go back to such a simple system [medieval production]... On the other hand...the workman should again have control over his material, his tools, and his time; only that control must no longer be of the individual workman, as in the Middle Ages, but of the whole body of workmen. When the workers organise work for the benefit of the workers...they will once more know what is meant by art.[30]

But at the time the young Morris could only see the lightning and the conflagration. He had no idea that there was a possible future beyond the 'cash-nexus'. For a follower of Carlyle, Keats and Ruskin the choice was between the present and the past, or even dreams. Morris's instincts, even at this time, were good. He was right to assert that humankind had been degraded to the status of an appendage of a machine, that there was no longer pleasure in labour, that every human interaction, including art, was being turned into a balance sheet of financial profit and loss. He was anticipating the socialist principle that in a communist society there would not be the division between labour and play — the two would be the same.

So Morris's early position was both a retreat and an acceptance of rebellion. The alternative which enabled him to look to the future with hope was yet to come.

But for now Morris was to retreat into his 'holy warfare against the age'. In 1856 he left Oxford and returned to London to train as an architect. He wrote to a friend, 'I can't enter into politico-social subjects with any interest, for on the whole I see that things are in a muddle, and I have no power or vocation to set them right in ever so little a degree. My work is the embodiment of dreams in one form or another'.[31]

*M*ORRIS THE artist was a great success. The later idea that 'fitness for purpose' was central to art can be detected in Morris and the Arts and Crafts Movement he encouraged. He was attempting to say something new in the language of the old. As E J Hobsbawm says:

> This movement of artistic renovation specifically sought to restore the broken links between art and the worker in production, and to transform the environment of daily living... It inspired those who wished to change life.[32]

Central to Morris's artistic output was the setting up of The Firm. The company was co-founded in 1861 with a view to manufacturing crafts, decorative work, furnishings and interior design. Morris set about training himself to work in the manner of the medieval craft workers, painstakingly researching medieval processes. In contrast to this were the developments in design going on in Victorian society. The Victorian bourgeoisie marked its affluence through ornate posessions, interior decoration and furnishings, and an architecture that still dominates our major city centres, a constant reminder of its power and self-confidence. This architecture was influenced by scholarship and the increasing ability for travel abroad, reflected at first in a hodgepodge of style, from Greek to Gothic, Roman to Byzantine. Manufacturing processes were revolutionised by the capacity for mass production — a further move away from the hand wrought product of the craftsman.

The 1851 Great Exhibition was held to celebrate the British Empire. Morris's friend and contemporary Walter Crane described the exhibits as 'monstrosities in furniture and decoration which were supposed to be artistic'. The exhibition was housed in the marvel that was the Crystal Palace, which was in itself an indication of the impact of increasing industrialisation — that it was possible to throw up huge prefabricated buildings in a short space of time. Morris earnestly swam against the tide, painstakingly trying to recover and perfect the skill of craftwork. He researched and tried to reproduce ancient dyes. His famous flower wallpaper patterns were handprinted. He wanted work to be enjoyable and satisfying. In the place of mass production he put the intricate and the finely finished. In place of outward show of wealth he put simplicity. As Morris said, 'I have never been in a rich man's house which would have not looked the better for having a bonfire made outside of it of nine tenths of all that it held'.[33]

Thus the motto he is best known for is, 'Have nothing in

your house that you do not know to be useful or believe to be beautiful.' The patterns that he created reflected his attitude to the world outside the door of his workshop. So his wallpaper patterns, 'Jasmine', 'Marigold', 'Apple' and 'Vine', were attempts to try and recreate an essence of the natural world outside the conurbations. As a visitor exclaimed, The Firm 'seems as if it were all-a-growing'. This fits with Morris wanting patterns to be a 'visible symbol' of nature, clothing 'our daily and domestic walls with ornaments that remind us of the outward face of the earth, of the innocent love of animals, or of man passing his days between work and rest'.[34]

Morris wanted this philosophy to be reflected in town planning. 'We must turn this land from the grimy backyard of the workshop into a garden.' Town architecture should 'to a certain extent make up to town dwellers for their loss of field, and river, and mountain'. He wanted housing to be built round existing trees instead of levelling everything until it was 'as bare as a pavement'. 'Every child should be able to play in a garden close to the place where his parents live.' Morris also advocated that housing should be social. It could be built:

In tall blocks, in what might be called vertical streets, but that need not prevent ample room in each lodging, so as to include such comforts of space, air and privacy as every moderately-living middle class family considers itself entitled to... Inside the houses, beside such obvious conveniences as common laundries and kitchens, a very little arrangement would give the dwellers in them ample and airy public rooms in addition to their private ones; the top storey of each block might well be utilised for such purposes, the great hall for dining in, and for social gathering, being the chief feature of it.[35]

This is Morris at his very best, visionary in his insights and practical in his views (apart from perhaps the communal dining halls!). If only the town planners who changed the skyline irrevocably in the second half of the 20th century had truly implemented Morris's vision.

During this period (roughly from 1856 to 1884) Morris increasingly came up against a contradiction that eventually drove him into political action. This was the contradiction between the past he revered and the actual society he lived in. There was no real escape and nowhere to hide. It confronted him in his art. For instance in architecture he realised it was not so easy to revive or recreate Gothic style. As biographer Paul Thompson has written:

> A Gothic architect was forced continually to correct and oppose the habits of the mason, the joiner, the cabinet-maker, the carver etc, and to get them to imitate painfully the habits of the 14th century workmen, and to lay aside their own habits, formed not only from their own personal daily practice, but from the inherited turn of mind and practice of body of more than two centuries.[36]

It would be wrong to say that Morris wanted to slavishly recreate Gothic art and architecture. What was important was embodied in the process of mastering past skills, whether that be book binding, glass firing, engraving or weaving. It was the manner of the work, bringing out the creativity of the worker that was central to his medievalism.

This meant that the processes he used for manufacturing his furnishings cost a lot of money. He was forced to build up very rich clients, people who symbolised everything he detested. But to make his handicraft cheaper and thus more widely available would mean surrendering to mass production — separating the worker from his or her work. This too went against Morris's philosophy.[37]

So he was caught. He expressed this contradiction in typically rebellious and impatient fashion. He lost a contract for work for a church to provide a silk and gold altar cross after he included the following note with the estimate: 'Note: in consideration of the fact that the above item is a wholly unnecessary and inexcusable extravagance at a time when thousands of poor people in this so-called Christian country are in want of food — additional charge to that set forth above, ten pounds'.[38] Morris must have been infuriated when his contempt for his clients only served to make him even more fashionable to the rich. As a friend remarked, 'Top's very eccentricities and independent attitude towards his patrons seem to have drawn patrons around him'.[39] (Morris was nicknamed Topsy because of his mop of hair, the name borrowed from a character in the popular anti-slavery novel *Uncle Tom's Cabin*.)

It was ironic that the 'exquisite despair' of his poetry of the time, such as his famous collection *The Earthly Paradise*, was embraced by the middle classes as a retreat from the worst aspects of the society that they simultaneously upheld. During the 1870s Morris also began to travel to Iceland, fleeing a society that was overwhelming him to a pre-industrial country where everything, from the landscapes to the human relations seemed, at least to the traveller, unspoilt. He immersed himself in Nordic folklore and attempted to bridge the gap by exploring the nature of Victorian society through this medium. His poem *Sigurd the Volsung* (1876) replaced the romance between the traditional characters and made lust for gold the motivating force.

Benjamin Disraeli

In Victorian society Morris was increasingly a success, feted as a great poet and patronised by society's most prominent members. Yet the more success he attracted, the more unsatisfied he became. His discontent drove him to begin to intervene in society. His first public stand was, not surprisingly, a mixture of art and politics. In 1876 he founded the Society for the Protection of Ancient Buildings or Anti-Scrape, as it became known. This was launched to stop crude Victorian restoration (or mutilation as he saw it) of ancient monuments and buildings. He wrote to his prominent friends and influential figures to back Anti-Scrape. He drew on Ruskin for his manifesto: 'Take proper care of your monuments, and you will not need to restore them...and many a generation will still be born to pass a way beneath its shadow'.[40] However, this campaign served only to intensify his anger, not dampen it.

Then at the end of October 1876 a letter of protest arrived at the *Daily News*: 'Sir, I cannot help noting that a rumour is about in the air that England is going to war; and that from the depths of my astonishment I ask, On behalf of whom? Against whom? And for what end?'[41] The correspondent was William Morris, fulminating in fine rhetoric style at the prospects of Britain supporting Turkey in its war against Russia — a war that was part of the Eastern Question. The letter continued, 'I am writing this as one of a large class of men — quiet men, who usually go about their own business, heeding public matters less than they ought, and are afraid to speak in such a huge concourse as the English nation, however much they may feel, but who are now stung into bitterness by thinking how helpless they are in a public matter that touches them so closely'.[42]

The letter marked Morris's launch into politics. 'Stung' into action at the age of 43 he finally abandoned his retreat from the age in which he lived. Morris joined the movement against (self-interested) British intervention on the side of the fading Turkish Ottoman Empire against the Russian Tsarist Empire. In 1876 the Tory government of Benjamin Disraeli was thrown onto the defensive over its support for Turkey and securing of interests in the region, including, crucially, control of the key strategic trade route of the Suez Canal.

It was news of Turkish atrocities against the Christian population of Bulgaria that crystallised opposition against Disraeli. Liberal leader in opposition William Gladstone wrote a pamphlet, *The Bulgarian Horrors and the Question of the East*. It sold almost 250,000 copies in the space of a month. Morris weighed in against Disraeli, siding with Gladstone's position. The Victorian England that Morris detested was also the Victorian England of the empire.

The dominant idea in British society was that the empire was a God given right and that prosperity at home depended on expansion abroad. It led to the encouragement of a nationalism which aimed 'to resist, expel, defeat, conquer, subject or eliminate "the foreigner"'.

The ruling class knew that it had to try and wed a British working class that had a fine tradition of internationalism to its expansionist order. As socialist historians A L Morton and George Tate wrote:

> An ideology of imperialism was now developed to try to justify and win popular support of acquiring and penetrating overseas areas... Scientific theories, such as Darwinism, were perverted into its service. British history was rewritten in its image. Song writers, journalists, academics, clergy, poets joined in its new eulogy. By every means, imperialism was propagated as the new British orthodoxy.[43]

To stand out against chauvinism and imperialism, as Morris and others did, was incredibly important. Workers, organised into Radical Clubs up and down the country, pressed the Liberal Party to form a league against British imperialism. This became the Eastern Question Association (EQA) organised by Sheffield Radical Liberal MP, A J Mundella, with Morris on board as treasurer. Mundella acted as a fixer for Gladstone, his job being to provide a link between the working class and the Liberal Party establishment. Gladstone backed the EQA, hoping that he would ride back into office on the back of popular opposition to Disraeli's interventions. It was a purely opportunist move, as Morris was to find out to his cost.

For Morris this was to be a profound turning point, because for the first time in his life he was to encounter the organised working class. On 24 April 1877 Russia declared war on Turkey. That night Morris hurried to a meeting of the Workmen's Political Associations and Trade Societies, remarking afterwards that he was impressed by those workers who 'spoke well' on the issue.[44] Morris was beginning to address the contradiction that had driven him up to that point — wanting a better society but forced to retreat by evoking the past through lack of an agency of change.

In May 1877 Morris published his famous *Manifesto to the Working Men of England*. The focus for his powerful appeal is not the bishops, not the rich, the famous and the eminent — it is a direct address to the working class. It is a magnificent blast against the British establishment that up to then had regarded Morris as perhaps eccentric, but essentially one of them:

> Who are they that are leading us into war? Let us look at these saviours of England's honour, these champions of Poland, these scourges of Russia's iniquities! Do you know them? Greedy gamblers on the stock exchange, idle officers of the army and navy (poor fellows!), worn-out mockers of the Clubs, desperate purveyors of exciting war-news for the comfortable breakfast tables of those that have nothing to lose by war, and lastly, in the place of honour, the Tory Rump, that we fools, weary of peace, reason and justice, chose at the last election to 'represent' us: and over all their captain, the ancient place-hunter, who, having at last climbed into an earl's chair, grins down thence into the anxious face of England (Disraeli, recently made earl), while his empty heart and shifty head is composing the stroke that will bring on our destruction perhaps, our confusion certainly. O shame and double

shame, if we march under such a leadership as this in an unjust war against a people who are not our enemies, against Europe, against freedom, against nature, against the hope of the world.[45]

This was a powerful attack on the jingoism being whipped up by Disraeli and the Tories. But Morris's commitment was not returned by Gladstone and the Liberal Party in anything like equal measure. As war got closer, Disraeli, overtly backed by Queen Victoria, went on the attack by playing up anti-Tsarist feeling, mobilising the press against the EQA and encouraging right wing gangs to smash up anti-war meetings. Gladstone, seeing that there was no longer electoral advantage in the EQA, in a cowardly act dropped the campaign, leaving Morris and working class activists to face the rising jingoism on their own.[46]

Here was a bitter lesson to learn, and learn it Morris and others did: the Liberal Party, even with its radical wing, could not be a vehicle for working class interests. He was ever after warning against what he saw as the false promises peddled by Radical politicians, whom he accused of wilfully leading their supporters down 'a blind alley with nothing but a blank wall at the other end'.[47]

There was a crying need for an independent working class organisation. Morris was disheartened but not defeated. Not a natural public speaker, he began to lecture on art, but now fusing his long held artistic critique with his awakening opposition to imperialism. There is no doubt that his anti-imperialism is one of his finest contributions to socialist politics.

In a Birmingham meeting in 1879 he impressed his audience with the point that 'while we are met here in Birmingham to further the spread of education in art, Englishmen in India are...actively destroying the very sources of that education — jewellery, metal-work, pottery, calico-printing, brocade weaving, carpet-making — the famous and historical arts of their great peninsula have been...thrust aside for the advantage of any paltry scrap of so-called commerce'.[48] A year later he is even more explicit:

> England's place — what is England's place? To carry civilisation throughout the world? Yes indeed the world must be civilised, and I doubt not that England will have a large share in bringing about that civilisation... I begin to doubt if civilisation itself may not be sometimes so adulterated as scarcely to be worth the carrying — and how it cannot be worth much, when it is necessary to kill a man in order to make him accept it.[49]

Morris was searching around for a socialist organisation. In 1879 he became treasurer of the National Liberal League, formed to help working class people become Liberal candidates, but he found once again that principle was secondary to the elevation of Gladstone's fortunes. Then two years later he helped set up a shortlived Radical Union, an amalgam of London working class groups in which he hoped to organise a 'strong political party out of the Radical elements or out of the trade unions'.

Gladstone was back in office. The author of *The Bulgarian Horrors* now refused to reverse Disraeli's annexation of the Southern African Transvaal, passed the notorious 1881 Coercion Bill against Ireland's independence, and ordered the shelling of Alexandria by British warships during the Stockjobbers' Egyptian War. It confirmed for Morris his hatred of the intrigue and corruption of the 'wretched little personalities' that populated parliamentary politics and fuelled his revulsion for a system that nurtured itself through imperialism and war.

By now Morris was desperate to 'join any body who distinctly call themselves socialist'.

1   Quoted in E P Thompson, *William Morris: Romantic to Revolutionary*, Merlin Press, 1976, p684.
2   *William Morris Political Writings: Contributions to Justice and Commonweal 1883-1890* edited by Nicholas Salmon, Thoemmes Press 1994, p225.
3   *Political Writings of William Morris*, edited by A L Morton, Lawrence & Wishart 1979, p153.
4   Nicholas Salmon, op cit, p382.
5   A L Morton, op cit, p123.
6   In his lifetime Morris was considered for the position of poet laureate (but he couldn't stand the idea of composing fawning verses for royalty — a trap the present poet laureate has not escaped!).
7   Nicholas Salmon, op cit, pp37-38.
8   Ibid, p458.
9   All quotes from the 'Kingdom of Necessity to the Kingdom of Freedom: Morris's News From Nowhere', by Paul O'Flinn in *International Socialism 72,* 1996
10 E P Thompson, op cit p732.
11 Paul Thompson, *The Work of William Morris,* Oxford University Press, 1993, p71.
12 Nicholas Salmon, op cit, p234.
13 E P Thompson, op cit, p2.
14 John Saville, *The Consolidation of the Capitalist State*, Pluto Press, 1994, see Introduction.

15 A L Morton, and George Tate, *The British Labour Movement: 1770-1920,* Lawrence and Wishart, 1956, p101.
16 William Morris quoted in John Bellamy Foster, Marx's Ecology, Materialism and Nature, *Monthly Review Press,* New York page 237
17 A L Morton and George Tate, op cit, p106.
18 Frederick Douglass quoted in Terry Allen, Blacks in Britain, University of Rochester Frederick Douglass Project, *www.lib.rochester.edu/index.cfm?PAGE=2509*
19 The lack of struggle has in the past been put down to a 'labour aristocracy' of the upper layer of skilled workers (maybe 15 percent of the working class) who supposedly benefited from British capitalism to such an extent that they became a conservative block against the working class movement. However, this notion has been increasingly challenged and, in short, though there was an upper layer of better paid skilled workers who regarded themselves as 'respectable' and apart from the unskilled worker, this is a far cry from an 'aristocracy'. The failure of Chartism, and a break in the radical tradition of workers (not least by imprisonment and transportation) combined with an expanding economy and the ability to fight for better conditions within the framework of capitalism, and a ruling class able to make concessions is a much more convincing explanation of the relative lack of struggle between the 1850s and the 1880s. It is also important to note that the leaders of New Unionism in the 1880s were people like Tom Mann and John Burns, who had both been engineers. For more on this see article by K Corr and A Brown on 'The Labour Aristocracy and the Roots of Reformism' in *International Socialism 59* (London, 1993).
20 A few were allowed to stand as 'Lib-Lab' candidates in parliamentary elections as a reward for delivering working class votes to the Liberal Party. So, for instance, miners' leaders Alexander MacDonald and Thomas Burt were elected as Lib-Labs in Stafford and Morpeth in 1874, having been given a free run against the Tories. MacDonald was not even on the Radical wing of the Liberals. He was described as 'almost a parable of Victorian thrift, diligence and self-help'.
21 Nicholas Salmon, op cit, p551.
22 A L Morton, op cit, p29.
23 *Selected Letters of John Keats*, edited by Grant F Scott, Harvard University Press, 2002, p49

24 A L Morton, op cit, p29.

25 Ibid, p14.

26 John Ruskin, The Nature of Gothic, in *On Art and Life* Penguin Great Ideas series, p15.

27 Frederick Engels, *Socialism: Utopian and Scientific*, Bookmarks, 1993, p78.

28 Nicholas Salmon, op cit, p20.

29 Frederick Engels, op cit, p92.

30 Nicholas Salmon, op cit, p20.

31 E P Thompson, op cit, p40.

32 E J Hobsbawm, *The Age of Empire 1875-1914*, Abacus, 1994, p229.

33 E P Thompson, op cit, p98.

34 Ibid, p105.

35 Ibid, p71.

36 Ibid, p62.

37 It would be wrong to say that Morris was totally against new machine techniques — he regretted that 'in my small business I am obliged to refrain from doing certain kinds of weaving I should like to do because my capital can't compass a power loom. (quoted in Paul Thompson, op cit, p104). Rather he felt he couldn't get the quality he needed from the machines that were around at the time. He also sold Arthur Gaskin's machine made teapots, kettles and fittings in the Firm's show rooms.

38 E P Thompson, op cit, p249.

39 Ibid, p109.

40 Fiona MacCarthy, *William Morris: A Life For Our Time* (Faber & Faber, 1994), p376.

41 Ibid, p380.

42 Ibid, p380.

43 A L Morten and George Tate, op cit, p140.

44 Fiona MacCarthy, op cit, p381.

45 E P Thompson, op cit, p214.

46 A L Morton, op cit, p47

47 At the time Marx and others on the left took a different attitude to the Eastern Question. Marx did not support a movement that gave backing to the Russian ruling class either militarily or politically, while

being clear that he in no way backed Disraeli's imperialism. Russia under the Tsar was a bastion of reaction. Marx considered a weakened Tsar would be to the advantage of the working class movement in Russia and elsewhere.
48 E P Thompson, op cit, p260.
49 Ibid, p260.

Part 2

*Socialist League membership card 1890
signed by William Morris*

*I*N THE WINTER of 1882 William Morris attended a series of lectures in central London organised by the Democratic Federation entitled 'The Stepping Stones to Socialism'. On January 1883 he joined the Federation and plunged himself into the study of Marxism. In the 13 years that followed he was to find himself at the centre of building the British Marxist tradition – agitating, organising, fighting, writing and lecturing, and leaving us with an enduring legacy. Morris's career proves that Marxism, not reformism, was the driving force at the centre of the British socialist movement from the start. Indeed those individuals who were in the forefront of the struggle in the decades that followed were schooled first in the ideas of Marxism by Morris and his contemporaries.

Interest in socialism had been kept alive in Britain since Chartism by the small London grouping around Marx and Engels. The 1871 Paris Commune provided embryonic proof that a socialist way of running society was possible and reawakened working class ideas in Britain with Republican Clubs springing up everywhere.[1] Through the late 1870s and 1880s there was the establishment of working class associations in the East End of London that adhered to socialist ideas, membership being a mixture of local workers, Radicals, political refugees from Europe and former Chartists. There were parallel organisations beginning to come together elsewhere. The Midland Social Democratic Association in Birmingham was one example. Similar formations were emerging across Europe, North America and some of the colonies.

The Democratic Federation was launched by H M Hyndman, formerly a Tory Radical. Hyndman was a strange figure to be in at the beginning of British Marxism. He was a rich factory owner who had been a bit of an adventurer before taking up Marxism – globetrotting, journalism and making money on the stock exchange being among his pursuits. (He lost a part of his fortune at the first Barings bank crash in 1890.) His politics were a mixture of determinist Marxism and opportunist action. He believed the colonies to be 'the special heritage of the working class' – in contradiction to Morris's internationalism. He had to be persuaded out of opposition to Home Rule for Ireland which was the touchstone for all progressives. He wanted an expanded navy to 'keep command of the narrow seas and trade routes' to protect British interests. Yet in 1880 he read Marx's *Capital* (in French; it did not appear in English until 1887) and announced his conversion to socialism. At the founding of the Democratic Federation he presented the delegates with a copy of *England For All*, his pocket version of *Capital*. (He earned Marx and Engels' anger and suspicion for plagiarising Capital without any acknowledgement — he apparently thought Marx's name too German!). The Russian revolutionary leader V I Lenin gave a very good description of Hyndman as an 'English bourgeois philistine who, being the best of his class, finally finds the road to socialism for himself, but never completely throws off bourgeois views and prejudices'.[2]

Hyndman's crude interpretation of Marx's work led him to believe that socialism was inevitable and not far off, and the sole role of revolutionaries was to propagandise for it. As a contemporary described it, a future crisis would lead to a workers' uprising and the SDF (as it became) 'would resolve itself into a Committee of Public Safety, and...it would be for him as chairman of that body to guide the ship of state into the calm haven of socialism'.[3] Therefore any struggle short of revolution was a diversion from this. So he held that strikes merely renegotiated the level of exploitation:

> There is nothing in strikes themselves, whether for a rise of wages for all, or for the enactment of a minimum wage for the lowest grades of labour in any industry, which can emancipate the propertyless workers, or render them less dependent upon the owning and employing class. On the contrary, the most successful strikes under existing conditions do but serve to rivet the chains of economic slavery, possibly a trifle guilded, more firmly on their limbs.[4]

This was not Morris's position. He recognised that mass strikes had the potential to become 'a revolt against oppression: a protest against the brute force which keeps a huge population down in the depths of the most dire degradation, for the benefit of the knot of profit-hunters...a strike of the poor against the rich'.[5]

Marx and Engels in London would have nothing to do with Hyndman. Engels condemned him as a 'petty and hardfaced John Bull' and accused him of trying to 'buy up the movement'. Yet for all distortions of this 'weak vessel', as Marx put it, Hyndman and his voluminous writings attracted workers and intellectuals to Marxism.

Hyndman's works such as *Socialism and Slavery*, *The Historical Basis of Socialism in England* and *The Coming Revolution in England* popularised Marxism beyond a narrow circle of committed adherents. Crucially, the Democratic Federation was formed as British capitalism began to go into an economic crisis, feeding into discontent that began to stir itself in the working class for the first time since Chartism.

It is important to point out, without accepting Hyndman's ideas, that revolutionaries at the time were engaged in pioneering work. They were trying to apply a new set of ideas in a world that was changing at a rapid rate. Apart from the Paris Commune there was no example of how socialism could come about. The Russian Revolution of 1905 and the Bolshevik Revolution of 1917 were in the future. There was little experience of relating to trade unions and the day to day struggle of workers against capitalism. Relating to New Model Unions such as the ASE must have been a daunting task for socialists. Nonetheless the Democratic Federation made faltering, unsure steps towards workers.

The communist historian E J Hobsbawm in his 1961 essay 'Hyndman and the SDF', reassessing the historic role of the organisation, pointed out:

> Its greatest achievement was to provide an introduction to the labour movement and a training school for a sucession of the most gifted working class militants: for John Burns, Tom Mann and Will Thorne, for George Lansbury and

even for Ernest Bevin. Consequently also, in spite of its frequent neglect of trade unionism, its members or those formed in its school were at their most effective as trade union leaders.[6]

But in all, the sum of the people, including Morris, who passed through its ranks was greater than the contribution of the organisation itself.

The series of meetings that Morris attended, the 'stepping stones to a happier period', were an instinctive attempt to unite theory and practice. From the stepping stones conference came a series of immediate demands designed to bridge the gap between the goals of socialists and the aspirations of workers. The programme demanded 'the compulsory construction of public bodies of healthy dwellings for the people', 'free secular and technical education', legislation for an eight hour day, cumulative taxation of incomes over £300, public work for the unemployed, the repudiation of the national debt, state appropriation of the railways, the municipal ownership of gas, electricity and water supplies, and nationalisation of the land.[7]

The Federation endeavoured to unite existing organisations. So it soon had influence in the Land Reform Union and the National Secular Society. It gained the affiliation of the important Scottish Land and Labour League (co-founded in Edinburgh by Marx's old friend the Austrian socialist Andreas Scheu). Morris was enthused by his discovery of the Federation and of Marxism. By May 1883 he was on the Democratic Federation executive (he was predictably made treasurer due to his income and thereafter substantially subsidised the movement).

He made a serious study of Marx's writings. In *How I Became a Socialist* he describes how 'I put some conscience into trying to learn the economical side of socialism, and even tackled Marx, though I must confess that, whereas I thoroughly enjoyed the historical part of *Capital*, I suffered agonies of confusion of the brain over reading the pure economics of that great work'.[8]

This self-deprecating aside has been unfairly used to assert that Morris had no time for Marxist theory, implying that he was indifferent or even hostile to Marx's teachings. One biographer draws on a comment by Morris's daughter May, 'who watched his struggles, commenting perceptively that it was difficult for someone with her father's deeply emotional attitude to the people and the land to delve with sustained enthusiasm into the intricacies of the scientific socialism of Marx with its hard technical arguments and economic formulas'.[9]

This view can only be seriously sustained if one discounts the whole of Morris's political trajectory from 1883 to his death. He demonstrated his rounded knowledge of Marxism through and through, whether writing about art, workers' struggles or history. As E P Thompson argued:

> No one familiar with socialist theory can doubt that Morris stood within the Marxist tradition... The evidence is to be found, not in coloured reminiscences or second-hand opinions, but in Morris's own political writings. The whole of Morris's socialist writing is rich in illustrations of class struggle. This, indeed, was to him the point of prime importance, distinguishing revolutionary socialism from reformism.[10]

Socialism From the Root Up, which he co-wrote with fellow socialist Belfort Bax, was an attempt to openly explain *Capital* to a working class audience. *A Dream of John Bull* was an attempt to explain the theory of historical materialism which argues that human beings make history, but not in conditions they choose – that they are simultaneously products of the age in which they live but not prisoners of it.

Morris, through his public speaking and writing, turned out to be one of the finest recruiting sergeants to Marxism that the British working class ever had. Again, writing in *How I Became a Socialist*, he asserted, 'The consciousness of revolution stirring amidst our hateful modern society prevented me, luckier than many others of artistic perceptions, from crystallising into a mere railer against "progress" on the one hand [like Ruskin], and on the other from wasting time and energy in any of the numerous schemes by which the quasi-artistic of the middle classes hope to make art grow when it has no longer any root, and thus I became a practical socialist'.[11]

Morris distanced himself from the doctrine of reformism, not because he opposed gradual change per se, but because reformism as a political programme rarely did what it said on the label — delivered true reforms for the mass of people.

> I hold that we need not be afraid of scaring our audiences with too brilliant pictures of the future of society, nor think ourselves unpractical and utopian for telling them the bare truth, that in destroying monopoly we shall destroy our present civilisation. On the contrary, it is utopian to put forward a scheme of gradual logical reconstruction of society which is liable to be overturned

at the first historical hitch it comes to; and if you tell your audiences that you are going to change so little that they will scarcely feel the change, whether you scare any one or not, you will certainly not interest those who have nothing to hope for in the present society, and whom the hope of a change has attracted towards socialism. It is a poor game to play (though he often played in politics) to discourage your friends in order to hoodwink your foes for a brief space.[12]

One can have a good guess as to what Morris might have thought of today's New Labour word-twisting where 'reforms' have come to mean their very opposite.

It was anger at Victorian society that drove him to socialism, but it was the realisation that opposition to the system in itself was not enough that shaped him into a committed Marxist. Morris may have been 'a catch' for the SDF, but his discovery of Marxism enraged the establishment. For at exactly the same time as Morris became a revolutionary an as yet unaware British establishment was preparing the rituals for him to be sanctified as an eminent Victorian.

In July 1883 he was received as a Fellow of Exeter College, Oxford. Just four months later he returned to Oxford to deliver a speech on politics to Liberal and Radical minded undergraduates. Hyndman had been refused a platform but Morris was allowed to speak, on the misunderstanding that he was a moderate alternative. In the audience was John Ruskin. Morris delivered a storming critique of capitalism, including an extraordinary denunciation of the cruelty of war:

> I tell you that the very essence of competitive commerce is waste; the waste that comes of the anarchy of war. Do not be deceived by the outside appearance of order in our plutocratic society. It fares with us as it does with the older forms of war, that there is an outside look of quiet wonderful order about it; how neat and comforting the steady march of the regiment; how quiet and respectable the sergeants look; how clean the polished cannon; neat as a new pin are the storehouses of murder; the books of the adjutant and sergeant as innocent-looking as may be; nay, the very orders for destruction and plunder are given with the quiet precision which seems the very token of a good conscience; this is the mask that lies before the ruined cornfield and the burning cottage, the mangled bodies, the untimely death of worthy men, the desolated home.[13]

After Morris had finished there was a 'deathly hush'.

The college authorities were shocked, the newspapers went for him — he had to weather 'a sort of storm of newspaper brickbats'. The newspapers responded at first with obvious confusion at the fiery rhetoric of this eminent public figure: the *Manchester Weekly Times* hoped 'that he would reconsider his ideal, and have something less impracticable and less discouraging to say to us the next time'. A year later in the *London Echo* curiosity had turned to hostility: 'Mr Morris... is not content to be heard merely as a voice crying in the wilderness... He will be content with nothing less than the propagation of his ideas by means that must result in social revolution'.[14] As E P Thompson comments:

> After each lecture there would follow indignant letters to the local papers, and measured reproofs upon the

'unpractical', 'misguided idealist', 'poet-upholsterer', and so forth, swelled to a crescendo the moment that Morris had found a practical remedy to the evils which he had before attacked, and had proclaimed himself to be a member of a practical revolutionary movement.[15]

Morris was not deterred by this approbation. In 1883 he spoke in Manchester, Birmingham, Oxford, Cambridge and numerous lectures in London, exclusively for the Democratic Federation. This is the Morris who a few years previously had described himself as a 'quiet man' 'afraid to speak'.

In 1883 the Democratic Federation adopted a specific socialist programme, widening nationalisation to all 'means of production, distribution and exchange'. Out of this came the Democratic Federation manifesto, *Socialism Made Plain*, which was a great success, selling 100,000 copies. By the end of the year the SDF had made headway, reporting branches in Newcastle and Liverpool, and having contacts in Bristol, Birmingham, Edinburgh and Nottingham. The Democratic Federation, through intervention in strikes, albeit for the purpose of propaganda, it found a wider influence. The receptiveness of active groups of workers to Marxism was demonstrated by the setting up of a branch in Blackburn after intervention in the 1884 cotton strike. Morris himself travelled to Blackburn and addressed the 1,500 strikers who had gathered in the biggest hall in the town to hear the socialist case.[16]

A good measure of support was the size of the March 1884 procession to Highgate Cemetery called by Hyndman on the first anniversary of Karl Marx's death. It attracted over 1,000 marchers, with another 3,000 or 4,000 onlookers at

Highgate. Around this time the Democratic Federation renamed itself the Social Democratic Federation.

Three months earlier the SDF had taken an important step forward. A feature of Chartism had been the appearance of independently produced newspapers such as the *Northern Star* and the *Poor Man's Guardian* that played a crucial role as news-gatherers, organisers and discussion forums to the movement. The SDF launched a weekly paper, *Justice — the organ of the Social Democracy*. As an observer at the founding editorial meeting recounted, Hyndman 'declared that humbug, political, social and scientific, would be exposed, art was to be emancipated (here Morris nearly shook his shaggy head off with approving nods) and the workers of the world would be united by means of a great free, independent press!'[17] It marked the beginning of an outpouring of socialist writing by Morris. Between 1884 and 1890, in the space of six years, Morris published no less than 500 signed articles, including poetry, prose, sketches, lectures, essays and columns. It also signalled a reawakening of Morris's creative energies. This period is his finest.

His contribution for issue one of *Justice*, although not weighty politically, is typically Morris. It is titled 'An Old Fable Retold'. The theme was on the pitfall of 'practical politics' ('impractical!' being the barb shot at the socialists by their ideological foes). In it the storyteller describes how:

> In the days before man had completely established his domination over the animal world, the poultry of a certain country, unnamed in my record, met in solemn conference in the largest hall they could hire for their money: the

period was serious, for it was drawing near Christmas, and the question of debate partook of the gravity of the times; for, in short, various resolutions, the wording of which has not come down to us, were to be moved on the all important subject, 'with what sauce shall we be eaten?' This debate goes on, says the narrator of the fable, until a 'middle-aged barn-door cock' gets up and explains: 'I don't want to be eaten at all; is it poss...'

The cock is howled down with cries of 'practical politics!' and he retires from the assembly. The meeting ends in harmony with a resolution agreed upon to be forwarded to the farmer's wife. The fable ends with: A rumour has reached us that while there were doubts as to the sauce to be used in the serving up, slow stewing was settled on as the least revolutionary form of cookery. Moral: Citizens, pray draw it for yourselves.[18]

Morris and the other members sold *Justice* where they could. 'The wholesale newsagents would not take the paper, so the Federation members began to sell it on the streets, traipsing through Ludgate Circus, Fleet Street and the Strand, shouting, '*Justice*, the organ of social democracy, one penny!' Morris was soon rather unwillingly catapulted into the leadership of the movement. Members of the SDF including Morris, Karl Marx's daughter Eleanor, her partner Edward Aveling and leading figures such as Belfort Bax had grown frustrated by the behaviour of the dictatorial and opportunistic Hyndman, who was apt to ignore party decisions with which he did not agree. A year after the split the SDF was to suffer a heavy blow when it was revealed that Hyndman had secretly accepted 'Tory gold' in return for putting up two candidates in the general election to split the Liberal vote and let the Tories in. Morris was particularly alarmed at Hyndman's sectarian attitude to those attracted to the Radical wing of the Liberals. He disagreed with Hyndman's 'perpetual sneers at, and abuse of the Radicals, who, deluded as we must think them, are after all the men from where our recruits must come'. Morris was vindicated when the Oxford Radical Club was argued over to a revolutionary socialist position.

The SDF split in December 1884. Morris and Eleanor Marx went to Frederick Engels for advice on how to form a new party — which became the Socialist League. Engels later wrote, 'The whole movement here is but a phantom, but if it is possible to draw into the Socialist League a kernel of people who have a good theoretical understanding, much will be gained for a genuine mass movement, which will not long be coming.' Engels regarded Morris, Bax and Aveling as 'the only honest men amongst the intellectuals – but men as impractical (two poets and a philosopher) as you could possibly find'.[19] But such are the unexpected tributaries through which the course of history is sometimes apt to run.

The Socialist League manifesto, written by Morris, with its famous address to the workers, was published in the first issue of the organisation's newspaper – *Commonweal* (Commonwealth) in February 1885 and was published, on Engels' advice, first monthly then weekly. The manifesto is a clear exposition of the socialist case. Importantly it contains a passage on women's liberation which reflected Morris's position: 'Our modern bourgeois property-marriage, maintained as it is by its necessary complement, universal venal prostitution, would give place to kindly and human relations between the sexes'.[20] Shot through Morris's writings is the issue of women's oppression. He was firm that he 'did not consider a man a socialist at all who is not prepared to admit the equality of women'.[21]

The manifesto also takes up the question of nationalisation: 'Whose aim it would be to make concessions to the working class while leaving the present system of capital and wages still in operation: no number of merely administrative changes, until the workers are in possession of all political power, would make any real approach to socialism'.[22] This passage also confirms that Morris was certain that the road to socialism would involve the 'dictatorship of the proletariat' — the seizing of state power — far from the ethos of gradualism that Morris is often tarred with today.

Morris was also at pains to make the point that the League was internationalist, against the chauvinism of Hyndman: 'For us neither geographical boundaries, political history, race, nor creed makes rivals or enemies; for us there are no nations, but only varied masses of workers and friends'.[23]

The first edition of *Commonweal* was an impressive effort. As well as the manifesto it had Belfort Bax on 'Imperialism Versus Socialism', Eleanor Marx on the international labour movement and reminiscences by the Chartist E T Craig of the Peterloo Massacre (In 1819 mounted yeomanry wrote a bloody page in the history books by attacking and killing unarmed pro-democracy demonstrators at St Peter's Fields in the centre of Manchester). This quality and breadth were kept up in following issues that included articles by Engels,

French socialist Paul Lafargue and playwright and scholar of Marxism George Bernard Shaw.

*I*n his writings for *Commonweal* Morris's clear-sighted analysis shines out. Take the issue of the divide and rule that propels modern racism: In 1886 Morris wrote an article entitled 'A Letter From The Pacific Coast' commenting on a report from a socialist living in San Francisco describing a recent conference called to discuss the position of Chinese labourers. The city's industrialists had cynically used the poorly paid Chinese to attempt to undermine the conditions other groups of workers. This had provoked a racist backlash and led to calls for the expulsion of Chinese workers from the city amid rumours of organised outbreaks of racist violence. The correspondent reported, however, that socialists had argued against this ugly mood: 'Our speakers declared (and we had the ear of the audience throughout) that the Chinaman was our brother-slave; that we had no quarrel with him, and that not one drop of his blood must be shed; that the crime lay with the property owners, the employers who make profit out of the Chinese'.[24]

Morris, after a tactical discussion of the issues involved, insightfully points out that the labour question in America had entered 'a new phase" and that it followed that new strategies to incorporate migrant workers into the trade unions had to be developed. He concludes:

> The Chinese workmen are only doing what every workman is forced to do more or less, that is to compete with his fellows for subsistence. It is true that the Chinese are forced by capital into being more obviously the

enemies of their fellow-workmen than is usually the case, but that is only a surface difference; it is more dramatic, that is all...If the American workmen can see this, and abstain...from playing into the hands of their real enemies by attacking their fellow wage-slaves the Chinese, they will deserve well of the Brotherhood of labour, and will show that they understand the motto: Wage-workers of all countries unite![25]

For the next six years Morris edited (and subsidised) *Commonweal*. The first issue sold around 3,500 copies, not a bad figure at all. It strove to connect with workers, and become a popular newspaper, as its promotional leaflets demonstrate: 'It speaks plainly without fear or favour on behalf of the suffering. It shows plainly your actual position... It tells you what you are, that is down-trodden slaves, and what you ought to be — the rulers of yourselves'.[26]

Morris wanted to build a revolutionary socialist party in the working class: 'When I first joined the movement I hoped that some working class leaders would turn up, who would push aside all middle class help, and become great historical figures'.[27] To that end he bent his considerable energies. Between 1884 and 1890 he addressed over 1,000 meetings across the country.

Working meticulously on his speeches Morris criss-crossed Britain by train, endeavouring to attract workers to the cause. Some of his most absorbing articles are reports from lecture tours and party organisational meetings. His report in *Commonweal* of a lecture tour in 1886, showing him involving himself in the nuts and bolts of organisation, is one of the many examples:

In Edinburgh: I had a short but pleasant interview with members of the branch... They seemed rather depressed: lack speakers, and so find it difficult to make much way; but they are getting a few new members, in spite of the slackness of their propaganda... On the other hand, our comrades are making most commendable efforts to push the *Commonweal*, and with it much success. The news shops take it and sell it.

The next day he is in Glasgow. He notes, 'Our comrades here ought to make a push and get up a branch in Dundee'.[28]

In the spring of 1887 the Socialist League made one of its first major interventions and showed what was possible for socialists to achieve at the time. Scottish Socialist League member and leading trade unionist John L Mahon had argued in the organisation for an orientation on strikes and the setting up of a 'strike committee'. In 1887 he established the North of England Socialist Federation among Northumberland miners. Morris suspected Mahon of trying to set up a new party entirely. But whatever Mahon's intentions, the result was a body that drew to it both members of the League and the SDF, prepared to work together without resort to the sectarian London based squabbles.

The Federation played a leading role in the 1887 Northumberland Great Miners' Strike against a 12.5 percent reduction in wages. Morris went up and spoke to a rally of 7,000 miners and their families. During the dispute the North of England Socialist Federation founded 24 branches and, although they faded away after the strike's settlement, they demonstrated the influence that socialists could win among workers. But apart from individuals such as Mahon, and later on members in Leeds, the Socialist League as an organisation failed to grasp the significance and nature of trade union intervention. Not until members like Eleanor Marx seriously took up the question of industrial work among the unskilled workers of the East End were the experiences of Northumberland to be repeated.

Meanwhile Morris and the League were plunged into campaigns for free speech involving joint work with wider forces than themselves. A crucial part of both the SDF's and the League's activities was selling their publications at street meetings. As E P Thompson writes, 'Morris would go with a few members of the League...to the stands of the Hammersmith branch [to which Morris belonged], at Waltham Green or Hammersmith Bridge, where audiences of up to 500 were regularly won'.[29]

Increasingly through the 1880s the London police harassed the small groups of socialists and Radicals, no doubt fearing the kind of solidarity they expressed with the Paris Commune of 1871. In the summer of 1885 the harassment was stepped up in the East End of London with socialists arrested every weekend. The SDF, the League and East End Radical Clubs came together to form a united front — the Free Speech Vigilance Committee — and called for a mass demonstration to be held on 20 September. This was attacked by the police, the socialist banner was seized and eight people were arrested. Then Morris himself was arrested when protests erupted outside the Thames police Court after the crowd heard that harsh sentences of hard labour had been handed down against the eight accused.

Morris was hauled off the pavement and into the dock. Accused of assaulting a police officer (pulling his helmet off) he was charged with a public order offence. However, the magistrate, a shamelessly biased figure named Saunders, being confronted by an indignant Morris, had the sense to drop the charges but only after this priceless courtroom exchange had been played out:

MR SAUNDERS: What are you?
PRISONER: I am an artist, and a literary man, pretty well known, I think, throughout Europe.
MR SAUNDERS: I suppose you did not intend to do this [strike the officer].
PRISONER: I never struck him at all.
MR SAUNDERS: Well, I will let you go.
PRISONER: But I have not done anything.
MR SAUNDERS: Well, you can stay if you like.
PRISONER: I don't want to stay.

He was then liberated, and on getting into the street was loudly cheered by the crowd.[30]

This episode scandalised Morris's respectable contemporaries — Morris, author of *The Earthly Paradise*, scuffling with the police and in the company of 'ruffians'! The writer George Gissing moaned, 'It is painful to me beyond expression. Why cannot he write poetry in the shade?... Keep apart, keep apart, and preserve one's soul alive — that is the teaching for the day. It is ill to have been born in these times, but one can make a world within a world'.[31]

Fortunately, others drew less supine conclusions. Among the working class the affair had the effect of widening opposition to the police; the following Sunday around 60,000 demonstrators took to the streets. The police were under orders to hold back (it was on the eve of a general election), and the socialists celebrated an important success. But the war was far from over.

The police, out to crush the movement, came back for more, notoriously on 13 November 1887, known as Bloody Sunday. A short revival of trade between 1881 and 1883 had alleviated unemployment. But this faded away, leaving a savage depression, throwing increasing numbers of people out of work. The recession crippled the by now 'fossilized' New Model Unions, whose funds were exhausted by unemployment benefits. Their strength, dependent on there being a shortage of labour, was transformed by the recession into their key weakness and they were soon to be overtaken by the militant 'New Unionism', led by fiery figures such as Tom Mann and John Burns who sought to mobilise the unskilled mass of workers in the gas industry, coal mines and docks. The response of the SDF to the rising ranks of the unemployed was to agitate among them (even to the extent of drilling them to get them in shape for the insurrection that Hyndman believed imminent). This agitation led to Black Monday in February 1885 when an SDF called demonstration in Trafalgar Square ended in a small riot after the demonstration was jeered and pelted by Pall Mall Club patrons. This took place against a background of unemployed riots in Leicester and elsewhere. The response of the SDF was to exaggerate this entirely as the signal for the coming revolution. They found themselves in agreement with Queen Victoria who complained that it was the 'momentary triumph of socialism and a disgrace to the capital'. Morris's analysis was more measured than the SDF's. In an editorial in *Commonweal* he wrote of these outbreaks of bitterness amongst the unemployed:

> What is to be said about these? They are leaderless often, and half blind...[but] the worse thing we have to dread, though every day now it is less to be dreaded, is that the oppressed people will learn a dull contentment with their lot, and give their masters no more trouble than dying inconveniently... With all genuine revolutionary attempts, therefore, we must sympathise, and must at the least express that sympathy.[32]

The response of the ruling class to Black Monday was twofold: subscriptions to the Mansion House Fund for the Unemployed, having hit rock bottom, rocketed, 'not out of pity but fear', as Hyndman wryly observed. Their other response was to look at what preparations they had for confronting working class revolt for the first time since Chartism. A new Metropolitan Police commissioner was swiftly appointed.

Sir Charles Warren had commanded the Diamond's Field Horse during the South African 'Kaffir War' of 1877-1878 and was feted as the 'Saviour of Bechuanaland'. One paper observed that he was more used to 'dealing with barbarians than the inhabitants of London', which is presumably why the then Tory administration picked him. His opinion of the unemployed soothed the bigots.[33]

The scene was set for confrontation. As Eleanor Marx wrote, 'In the streets here one sees so many starving people-people with hunger in every line of their faces that one cannot but be wretched'.[34] Trafalgar Square became the focus for the unemployed, many of whom had nowhere else to sleep. On Tuesday 8 November a public notice appeared in the newspapers, a declaration by Charles Warren that all meetings in Trafalgar Square were banned. But a rally in the square by the Metropolitan Radical Federation and the Irish National League in protest at renewed repression in Ireland and the internment of Irish MP William O'Brien was already planned. It now became the rallying point for free speech (thus converging the two great progressive causes of the day in much the same way as today's anti-war movement succeeded in uniting Muslims, the peace movement and socialists).

Bloody Sunday started with the occupation of the square by hundreds of police on foot, mounted police and foot soldiers of the Grenadiers and Life Guards while feeder marches assembled across London. In Clerkenwell Green, Morris and others addressed one contingent of 5,000. Morris knew that the authorities lay in wait. He reportedly warned the crowd, 'When the procession was passing through the streets, those behind must not fall back... He hoped they would shove the policemen, rather than hit them, for the policemen were armed and they were not'.[35]

The viciousness of the attack on the demonstrators was much worse than Morris imagined. He recounted in the next issue of *Commonweal*:

> We had no sooner crossed [Shaftesbury Avenue] than the attack came, and it was clearly the best possible place for it... It was all over in a few minutes: our comrades fought valiantly... The police struck right and left like what they were, soldiers attacking an enemy, amidst wild shrieks of hatred from the women who came from the slums on our

left. The band instruments were captured, the banners and flags destroyed, there was no rallying point and no possibility of rallying, and all that the people composing our once strong column could do was struggle into the square as helpless units. I confess I was astounded at the rapidity of the thing and the ease with which military organization got its victory... An eye-witness who marched up with the western column told me that they were suddenly attacked as they came out opposite the Haymarket Theatre, by the police rushing out on them from the side streets and immediately batoning everybody they could reach, whether they resisted or not. [36]

Morris was shocked and disgusted at the brutality of the attack which included 'one brave man wrapping his banner torn from his pole around his arm and facing the police till he was hammered down with repeated blows'.[37] The police eventually cleared the square through mounted baton charges. Two hundred demonstrators were hospitalised, two men dying shortly after as a result of their injuries. Three hundred were arrested, with 160 people sent to jail. The hundred odd police injuries were a testiment to the courage with which demonstrators attempted to fight back. The Law and Liberty League was launched shortly after to aid those arrested and injured. A 40,000 strong meeting in Hyde Park the following Sunday passed a resolution which demanded the release of those arrested, condemned Warren and demanded the right to assembly in the capital. Later, in Trafalgar Square, an innocent law clerk, Alfred Linnell, was killed by mounted police. On Sunday 18 December the working class of London turned out to mourn and vent their anger. A huge demonstration 120,000 strong marched the miles from central London to Bow cemetery. Morris had written the poem *A Death Song* for Linnell (see below page 127). It was produced as a penny pamphlet and sold on the march to raise money for Linnell's bereaved family:

> What cometh from west to east a-wending?
> And who are these, the marchers stern and slow?
> We bear the message that the rich are sending
> Aback to those who bade them wake and now.
> Not one, not one, nor thousands must they slay,
> But one and all if they would dusk the day.[38]

Morris gave the speech at the graveside:

> Our friend who lies here has had a hard life and met with a hard death, and if society had been differently constituted his life might have been a delightful, a beautiful and a happy one. It is our business to begin to organise for the purpose of seeing that such things shall not happen; to try and make this Earth a beautiful and happy place.

A comrade remembered how:

> He threw his whole soul into his speech. There was a fearful earnestness in his voice when referring to the victim he had just laid to rest. He cried out, 'Let us feel he is our brother.' The ring of brotherly love in it was most affecting.[39]

Despite Bloody Sunday and the death of Linnell the fight for free speech was successful – not only were the authorities forced to back down and concede the right of assembly in Trafalgar Square, but the struggle had also raised the profile of the socialists in the working class movement.

1   Eighty-four republican clubs were formed in Britain between 1871 and 1874.
2   Lenin quoted in A L Morton and George Tate, op cit p164.
3   E P Thompson, op cit, p295.
4   H M Hyndman, *Further Reminiscences* (Macmillan, 1912), p459.
5   A L Morton, op cit p432.
6   Eric Hobsbawm *Labouring Men: Studies in the History of Labour* (Weidenfield and Nicolson, 1986), p232. John MacLean also came into politics via the SDF.
7   Fiona MacCarthy, op cit, p472.
8   Ibid, p241.
9   MacCarthy has to admit that: 'He [Morris] persevered, and the following year was still carving out time from his onerous lecture tours and socialist committees to study Marx's theories of work and wages'. Ibid, p468.
10 E P Thompson op cit p682.
11 A L Morton, op cit, p341.
12 Nicholas Salmon, op cit, p341.
13 Ibid, p244.
14 Fiona MacCarthy op cit, p478.
15 E P Thompson, op cit, p309.
16 See Fiona McCarthy, op cit, p487.
17 Quoted E P Thomson, op cit 313.
18 Ibid, p3.

19 Fiona MacCarthy, op cit, p509.
20 E P Thompson, op cit, p735.
21 Paul Thompson, op cit, p251.
22 A L Morton, op cit, p118
23 Ibid p120-121
24 E P Thompson, op cit, p736.
25 Ibid, p732. Morris's opposition to racism also led him to appear in November 1890 on the platform at the International Working Mens Educational Club rally in Mile End in East London 'Against the Inhuman Treatment and Persecution of the Jews in Russia' alongside John Burns, Prince Stepniak, Eleanor Marx, Michael Davitt (Irish MP) and Cunningham Graham.
26 Fiona MacCarthy op cit, p514.
27 Nicholas Salmon, op cit, p490.
28 Quoted in E P Thompson op cit, p397
29 Ibid, p134.
30 E P Thompson, op cit, p394.
31 Fiona MacCarthy, op cit, p528.
32 Nicholas Salmon, op cit, p134.
33 See Rodney Mace, *Trafalgar Square-Emblem of Empire* (Lawrence and Wishart, 1976), p170.
34 Yvonne Kapp, *Eleanor Marx* vol 2 (Pantheon Books, 1976), p222.
35 Thompson, op cit, p489.
36 Nicholas Salmon, op cit, p303.
37 Ibid, p303.
38 MacCarthy, op cit, p573.
39 Ibid, p573.

Part 3

The birth of New Unionism with the Dockers' Strike 1889

William Morris worked ceaselessly throughout the hectic years of the Socialist League, editing, contributing to *Commonweal* and delivering lectures whenever or wherever they were needed. He was always at pains to address the questions thrown up by activists and those attracted to socialist ideas. He knew people wanted to go beyond what they were against, and they also had a thirst for ideas that articulated what they were for. This is reflected in the titles of his talks and articles – to audiences across Britain he spoke on subjects as 'A Factory as It Might Be'; 'Art and Socialism'; 'How We Live and How We Might Live'; 'The Hopes of Civilisation and The Society of the Future'.

There was one topic he took up time and again – the nature of work under capitalism and the potential for its transformation under a future socialist society.

In 1885 the Socialist League published a brief pamphlet culled from a lecture of Morris's entitled *Useful Work Versus Useless Toil*. In it he attempts to explain how present society 'alienates' us from what we produce and how this state of affairs would change fundamentally in a socialist society. He starts by pointing out that humanity has to labour to survive: 'Nature does not give us our livelihood gratis; we must win it by toil of some sort or degree'.[1] But there were different kinds of work, Morris explained: 'good' work - 'one not far removed from a blessing, a lightning of life' and 'bad' work – 'a mere curse, a burden to life'.[2] The difference between the two lay in what kind of work, and who and what it is was for. Morris explained that under capitalism there was a tiny 'class of rich people doing no work; we all know that they consume a great deal while they produce nothing'.[3] At the other end there was the working class, that 'produces all that is produced, and supports both itself and the other classes, though it is placed in a position of inferiority to them; real inferiority, mind you, involving a degradation of both mind and body'.[4] Morris observed that the majority are forced to produce 'articles of folly and luxury' for the rich non-producers (in which today we could include the destruction tied up in the manufacture of arms on a horrendous scale). The rich regard these articles as their 'wealth' but, as Morris points out, they represent waste. It is a world turned upside down, reflected in the way in which the meanings of words have been corrupted: The real meaning of 'wealth' asserts Morris is the opposite of riches and conspicuous consumption — surely it's real meaning 'is what nature gives us and what a reasonable man can make out of the gifts of nature for his reasonable use. The sunlight, the fresh air, the unspoilt face of the earth, food, rainment and housing necessary and decent; the storing up of knowledge of all kinds, and the power of disseminating it; means of free communication between man and man; works of art, the beauty which man creates when he is most a man, most aspiring and thoughtful – all things which serve the pleasure of people, free, manly and uncorrupted. This is wealth'.[5]

But for the majority there is no 'wealth' to be had. On top of fine luxuries for the rich, workers are forced to produce inferior goods for their own consumption – going against not only their need, but their human desire to produce decent things. Workers 'must put up with miserable makeshifts…with coarse food that does not nourish, with rotten rainment that does not shelter, with wretched houses which may make a town-dweller in civilisation look back with regret to the tent of the nomad tribe, or the cave of the pre-historic savage… The wage-earners must always live as the wage-payers bid them, and their very habits of life are forced on them by their masters'.[6]

Morris then points out the great contradiction under capitalism – that the system has developed, above any previous society, the ability to produce enough to satisfy our needs. We know today, for example, that we grow enough food to feed the world many times over, that we have the ability to build decent houses for all, and the science to rid us of common yet deadly diseases – 'But what is the real fact? Who will dare to deny that the great mass of civilised men are poor? So poor are they that is mere childishness troubling ourselves to discuss whether perhaps they are in some way a little better off than their forefathers'. Today we too live in these times, where the gap between the rich and poor is widening while social mobility narrows. And in a tilt at what we call consumerism today Morris says that 'for the most of us, civilisation has bred desires which she forbids us to satisfy, and so is not merely a niggard but a torturer also'.[7]

Consider the expensive goods dangled before us today and the 'bling' culture young people are supposed to admire and aspire to.

It is a cruel, unfair, exploitative, destructive world, Morris argues: 'The fruits of our victory over nature [have] been stolen from us, thus has compulsion by nature to labour in hope of rest, gain and pleasure been turned into compulsion by man to labour in hope — of living to labour!'[8]

He sees a solution to this state of affairs: 'The first step to be taken then is to abolish a class of men privileged to shirk their duties as men... All must work to their ability, and so produce what they consume'.[9] This economic and political revolution would in turn produce a revolution in the nature of work. Not only would society be rid of the profiteers at the top of society, but 'there will be no compulsion on us to go on producing things we do not want, no compulsion on us to labour for nothing; we shall be able calmly and thoughtfully to consider what we shall do with the wealth of our labour power'. In short Morris is arguing for a society organised democratically for need and not for profit.

Morris ventures into a description of how that new kind of society might operate — instead of the 'tyranny of profit-grinding' we might 'easily learn and practise at least three crafts'; there would be more time for leisure, and the space for people to explore art and culture, an expertise in a science or a branch of industry or of learning that interested them. Thus would people transform their relationship to 'work' and those around them. People would change as the new society grew. The world around us would be changed – for example (tackling a subject close to Morris's heart) 'the glorious art of architecture, now for some time slain by commercial greed, would be born again and flourish'. However, Morris was at pains to make an important point — that there was no blueprint for a future socialist society — he was convinced that liberation of the spirit would see a blossoming of potential that could not be guessed, looking as we do from the stunted vantage point of present society: 'We have no doubt of the transformation of modern civilisation into socialism, yet we cannot foretell definitely what form the social life of the future will take'.[10]

It is often said of Morris that he advocated taking production backwards to the medieval guilds and thus he was against mechanisation full stop. Although it is the case that he didn't particularly like factory mass production, Morris had a much more rounded approach than that usually attributed to him. In *Useless Work Versus Useless Toil* he carefully argues that 'our epoch has invented machines which would have appeared wild dreams to the men of past ages, and of those machines we have yet made no use'. He points out that it is clearly the case under capitalism that these 'labour saving' devices have not been used to relieve workers of the burden of long hours and repetitive labour, but used instead to deskill workers and to replace them by imposing what is today called 'modernisation' or 'rationalisation'. In contrast Morris can see how in a future socialist society machinery could be put to good use: 'In a true society these miracles of ingenuity would be for the first time used for minimizing the amount of time spent in unattractive labour, which by their means might be so reduced as to be but a very light burden on each individual'.[11] Morris ventures to say that he hopes after a time huge factories packed with machinery might become obsolete as humanity found different ways to produce what was needed. But he was also clear, despite his admiration for the guild system, that a communist society could not mean a forced return to a sort of Year Zero: 'We cannot turn our people back into Catholic English peasants and Guild craftsmen, or into heathen Norse bonders, much as may be said for such conditions of life'.[12]

Morris also considered where we work. In his essay *A Factory As It Might Be* Morris argued that factories themselves would change from ugly hated buildings in which people were forced to work to a environment where 'our factory will have other buildings…for it will need dining-hall, library, school, places for study of various kinds'.[13] Instead of works of art being gathered in exclusive galleries Morris had a vision that 'the highest of most intellectual art, pictures, sculptures, and the like' would 'adorn a true place of industry'.

It was this liberation from the drudgery and alienation of work under capitalism that for Morris would herald his lifelong desire - the union of labour and art. In his talk 'Art and Socialism' he starts from a damning critique of free market capitalism or 'commerce', as he termed it, under which the things which people make are treated as commodities, whose value is determined not by their intrinsic worth but by their position in the marketplace.

Morris argued that 'art' in Victorian society was something confined to the world of the 'well to do', but under socialism would become part of the fabric of everyone's life. If one looks at the visual arts industry today, it has been captured by a multinational profit-driven ethos, and fabulously wealthy art collectors who decide what is of value to the market and what is not. Patronage by rich men defines what art is produced in a manner that is anything but modern – if anything it corresponds with past societies where painters were in the service of the nobility and the courts of emperors, kings and popes. For Morris the revolutionising of humanity's relation to work could be described as 'the pleasure of life', and thus for him this 'social revolution [would] be the foundations of the re-building of the art of the people'.[14] As he also put it in an article in *Commonweal* in 1888, under socialism where people worked collectively for the common good, 'out of that free co-operation will spring the expression of individual character and gifts which we call art. Then those spinning jennies…will be used for producing yarns which we want, and not those yarns that we only want to sell'.[15]

In a way Morris was anticipating future events such as the Russian Revolution of 1917, the mass strikes in Italy in 1920 and France in 1968, all of which saw workers, having seized control over the factories, begin immediately to throw up unique organisations that reordered work to meet human need. Morris would have delighted in events of the Russian Revolution recounted by the journalist John Reed (the subject of Warren Beatty's film *Reds* made in 1986): 'There was a cotton factory in Novgorod which was abandoned by its owners. The workers – inexperienced in administration – took charge. The first thing they did was manufacture enough cloth for their own needs, and then for the needs of the other workers in Novgorod'.[16]

Morris was prophetic in his belief that as workers moved into challenging capitalism they would seize upon art – 'the worker will then once again begin to have a share in art, when he begins to see his aim clear before him – his aim of a share of real life for all men...when his struggle for that aim has begun'.[17]

One might imagine Morris's feeling of vindication in the following account of the audience at an opera performance held at the Great State Theatre in Moscow in February 1919:

> 'The Moscow plutocracy of bald merchants and bejewelled fat wives had gone. Gone with them were evening dresses and white shirt fronts. The whole audience was in the monotone of everyday clothes. The only contrast was given by a small group of Tartar women in the dress circle, who were shawled in white over head and shoulders, in the Tartar fashion. There were many soldiers and numbers of men who had obviously come straight from work... Looking from face to face that night I thought there were very few people in the theatre who had anything like a good dinner to digest. But, as for their keenness, I can imagine few audiences to which, from the actor's point of view, it would be better worthwhile to play'.[18]

In 1891 Morris articulated his vision of the fusion between labour and art exquisitely when he wrote, 'When people once more take pleasure in their work, when the pleasure rises to a certain point, the expression of it will become irresistible, and the expression of pleasure is art, whatever form it takes'.[19]

Morris was always on the lookout for artistic works that

exemplified his political philosophy and the aesthetic that flowed from it. In 1893 he wrote to Thomas Armstrong, who was director of the arts division of the South Kensington Museum (which is now the Victoria and Albert), requesting that he buy and display to the public what is known as the Ardabil carpet.

> I never saw such a design in my life... This is the chief reason that I wish to see it bought for the public. The design is of singular perfection; defensible on all points, logically and consistently beautiful, with no oddities or grotesqueries which might need an apology, and therefore most especially valuable for a museum, the special aim of which is the education of the public in art. The carpet as far as I can see is in perfectly good condition, and its size and splendour as a piece of workmanship do full justice to the beauty and intellectual qualities of the design.[20]

The carpet was later bought through public subscription and is displayed in the Victoria and Albert Museum today.

Morris's opening up of the discussion about the nature of the working class, labour and art was a revelation to a late 19th century Britain defined as 'the workshop of the world' where workers were perceived by the elite as brutes having nothing to offer beyond their labour power and inferior in their sensibilities and desires. As E P Thompson wrote: 'Morris's lectures tore down the precious veils before the palace of art...revealed the enormous reserves of creative energy in the people, and stimulated the discussion of cultural problems within the working class movement'.[21] Uniquely Morris was determined to take this argument to the people that mattered to him — the working class — and they welcomed it, as evidenced in this account published in the *Newcastle Chronicle* of an open-air speech he delivered to a mass rally of the striking Northumberland miners:

> [Morris] did not call the life of the working man, as things went, a tolerable life at all. When they had gained all that was possible under the present system, they still would not have the life which human beings ought to have. (Cheers.) That was flat. What was their life at best? They worked hard, day in and day out, without any hope whatever. Their work was to live to work, in order they might live to work. ('Hear, hear' and 'Shame'.) That was not the life of men. That was the life of machines…he wished that the men might have a life of refinement and education and all those things which made what some people call a gentleman, but what he called a man. (Cheers.) That was the victory he wished them.[22]

Alongside his lectures and journalism Morris produced three enduring socialist masterpieces during this period, all first serialised in *Commonweal*: *The Pilgrims of Hope* (April 1885 to June 1886), *A Dream of John Ball* (November 1886 to January 1887) and the evergreen *News from Nowhere* (January to October 1890).

The Pilgrims of Hope is a narrative poem that merges Morris's early days as a socialist with a defence of the 1871 Paris Commune. For Morris to choose to defend and celebrate the Commune would have scandalised his contemporaries. But he believed in revolution. As he wrote elsewhere, 'My belief is that the old order can only be overthrown by force'.[23] At the same time the spectre of the Commune 'frightened the wits' out of the ruling classes, as Eric Hobsbawm puts it. In the working class movement the attitude taken to the Commune became a dividing line.

The right wing trade union leaders who headed the New Model Unions deserted the First International set up by Marx and Engels, scared that they would be labelled as supporters of foreign revolutionary conspiracies.

In contrast defending the Paris Commune was a point of pride for socialists. As Morris wrote in a *Commonweal* article, 'We honour them as the foundation-stone of the world that is to be.' That is why he entitled the section in *The Pilgrims of Hope*, when his three protagonists travel to the Commune, 'A Glimpse of the Coming Day':

> So at last from a grey stone building we saw a great flag fly, / One colour, red and solemn 'gainst the blue of the springtide sky, / And we stopped and turned to each other, and as each at each did we gaze, / The city's hope enwrapped us with joy and great amaze.[24]

The Pilgrims of Hope is also worth reading for the fictionalised account it provides of Morris's early days in the movement:

> When I joined the communist folk, I did what in me lay / To learn the grounds of their faith. I read day after day / Whatever books I could handle, and heard about and about / What talk was going amongst them; and I burned up doubt after doubt, / Until it befell at last to others I needs must speak.[25]

In *A Dream Of John Ball* Morris drew on his knowledge of medievalism to deliver a modern history lesson. He took as his subject the Peasants' Revolt of 1381. The uprising, led by Wat Tyler, Jack Straw and the preacher John Ball, had marched on London, demanding an end to the poll tax levies on the poor to pay for foreign wars, and an end to the system of serfdom. Ball's legendary sermon at Blackheath, south London, included the provocative passage:

> 'When Adam delved and Eve span, who was then the gentleman? From the beginning all men by nature were created alike, and our bondage or servitude came in by the unjust oppression of naughty men. For if God would have had any bondmen from the beginning, he would have appointed who should be bond, and who free. And therefore I exhort you to consider that now the time is come, appointed to us by God, in which ye may (if ye will) cast off the yoke of bondage, and recover liberty'. [26]

After storming the Tower of London the rebels at first extracted concessions out of the young king Richard II, but, caught off guard, Tyler was murdered by the King's henchmen. The movement collapsed and Richard exacted a bloody revenge. John Ball was captured, put through a mock trial and then hung, drawn and quartered.

In a familiar device the narrator in *A Dream of John Ball* falls asleep in the present day and finds himself back in 14th century Kent. Morris wanted to use the poem to say something about the nature of struggle and the historical context in which it is waged. E P Thompson argues that Morris wanted to assert the necessity for a conscious agency of change — that change for the better would not just come about naturally, as it were. What individuals and movements did was not incidental to history — they were integral to it — shaping the future. This was a rejection of the spontaneity and evolutionary conception that dominated Hyndman's theory. As Morris wrote elsewhere, 'If the present state of society merely breaks up without a conscious effort at transformation, the end, the fall of Europe, may be long in coming, but when it does, it will be far more terrible, far more confused and full of suffering than the period of the fall of Rome'.[27] Here he was echoing the Marxist maxim that society does not always move forward, that it can be thrown backwards irrevocably, resulting in the mutual 'ruin of the contending classes'.

John Ball, having heard his terrible fate, asks what his role in history is, while trying to grapple with the knowledge given to him by his 19th century vision that the feudalism he is fighting in his present is conquered, but its conquest ushers in not an end to tyranny, but the inconceivable — a more terrible order of things — capitalism:

'Now I am sorrier than thou hast yet made me,' said he, 'for when once this is established, how then can it be changed? Strong shall be the tyranny of the latter days. And now me seems, if thou sayest sooth, this time of the conquest of the earth shall not bring heaven down to the earth, as erst I deemed it would, but rather that it shall bring hell up onto the earth. Woe's me, brother, for thy sad and weary foretelling! And yet saidst thou that the men of those days would seek a remedy. Canst thou yet tell me, brother, what that remedy shall be?'

'John Ball,' [the narrator replies] 'be of good cheer; for once more thou knowest, as I know, that the fellowship of men shall endure, however many tribulations it may have to wear through... The time shall come, John Ball, when that dream of thine that this shall one day be, shall be a thing that men shall talk of soberly, and as a thing soon to come about...thy name shall abide by thy hope in those days to come, and thou shalt not be forgotten'.[28]

The narrator 'pondered how men fight and lose the battle, and the thing they fought for comes about in spite of their defeat, and when it comes turns out not to be what they meant, and other men have to fight for what they meant under another name'.[29]

As Morris wrote elsewhere: 'The past is not dead, it is living in us, and will be alive in the future which we are now helping to make.' *A Dream of John Ball* was set in the past, but firmly rooted in Morris's struggle for the future.

Like all of Morris's writings, *A Dream of John Ball* is full of sensuous descriptions of people. In Morris's writing the female characters are often idealised, so in *John Ball* a female character is described as:

> Tall and strongly made, with black hair like her father, somewhat comely, though no great beauty; but as they met, her eyes smiled even more than her mouth, and made her face look very sweet and kind, and the smile was answered back in a way so quaintly like to her father's face, that I too smiled for goodwill and pleasure.[30]

To the contemporary reader these descriptions may read awkwardly, partly because of the language and partly because of a perceived coyness and sentimentalism. But what Morris was trying to do was reveal an essential 'goodness' in human relations — in contrast to the present society that bred alienation, oppression and ugly conflict between individuals. In his writings Morris tried to allude, as best as he was able, to a world where men and women would be 'free' to form 'genuine unions of passion and affection'.[31]

Today Morris's fictional writings are dismissed as the work of a utopian dreamer. Indeed his best known work, *News from Nowhere*, has been labelled a 'socialist fantasy'. It was written in response to a popular book by the American Edward Bellamy in 1888. Bellamy was an academic who disliked the effects that capitalism was having on humanity and wanted a much more rational society. As an intellectual he convinced himself that 'logic' argued by clever men like himself would win out and that capitalism would inevitably be superseded by socialism — because it was, after all, a much more reasonable state of affairs.

In *Looking Backwards* Bellamy's hero wakes up in Boston in the year 2000 and finds himself in a socialist society. How did this marvellous state of affairs come about? We are told that over time all the corporations and businesses came together into a single syndicate representing the people, to be conducted in the common interest for the common profit[32] (think Disney, Microsoft, Ford, Coca-Cola and British Aerospace). This state of affairs did not take 'great bloodshed and terrible convulsions. On the contrary there was absolutely no violence. The change had been long foreseen. Public opinion had become fully ripe for it, and the whole mass of the people was behind it. There was no more possibility of opposing it by force than by argument'.[33] In a neat and tidy turnaround monopoly capitalism would eliminate competition and transform itself into socialism. Crucially there would be no need for revolution when evolution would do the job.[34]

This assertion irritated Morris enough to write his creative counterblast, *News from Nowhere* (apparently while travelling to public meetings by train). For not only did Bellamy's work advocate support for those monopoly capitalists who represented everything Morris detested, it also advocated the notion that capitalism would somehow grow over into a more rational state. It dismissed the idea that there was or ever would be a confrontation between the classes which would ultimately have to be fought out. Bellamy, in conclusion, was predicting that the future of humanity was more akin to the actual life that middle class Bostonians (like Bellamy) enjoyed in 1888 than communist society. Morris wrote, 'A certain tincture of socialism...(generally very watery) is almost a necessary ingredient nowadays in a novel'.[35] But he had to admit that Bellamy's book was also popular among workers who were drawn to the socialist project: 'The success of Mr Bellamy's utopian book, deadly dull as it is, is a straw to show which way the wind blows'.[36]

Morris first took up the argument in a review of the book in *Commonweal*. He refuted the idea that change would come about in the way Bellamy described: 'He conceives of the change to socialism as taking place without any breakdown of that life, or indeed disturbance of it, by means of the final development of the great private monopolies'.[37] He then proceeded to write *News from Nowhere*, at the heart of which is a defence of revolution and revolutionary change.

This motivation disturbed Morris's first biographer, J W Mackail, who dismissed the book, saying, 'It is a curious fact that this slightly constructed and essentially insular romance has, as a socialist pamphlet, been translated into French, German and Italian, and has probably been read in more foreign countries than any of his more important works in prose or verse'.[38] (Mackail regarded Morris's socialism as a rather distasteful malaise, setting the tone for a myriad of revisionist biographies that continues today.)

Yet *News from Nowhere* was far from being a whimsy – in fact, as Morris was well aware, it rested upon a long tradition of the struggle of the disenfranchised and the dissenting to articulate a creative alternative vision to the times they lived in. It is fascinating to sketch out Morris's antecedents.

The desire for a better world – *Utopia* (No Place), as Sir Thomas More coined it in his classic tract - for most of human history lay within the paradigm that contrasted the misery of class society with an 'unobtainable dream' of equality, of plenty and of human pleasure denied. An early recorded example of this is the prose poem *The Land of Cockaigne* – versions of which appeared in various Western European countries in the Middle Ages. Cockaigne was supposed to be an 'earthly paradise' somewhere 'West Of Spain'. Some scholars have suggested that it may even have echoes of word-of-mouth interpretations of the descriptions of paradise described in the Qur'an.[39] The poem reflects the preoccupation of the serf against the oppressive and corrupt church. It is viciously anti-clerical and obsessed with having an abundance of food:

> That land of Cockaigne is marvellous!
> It also rains in those fair parts
> Custards, pancakes, pies and tarts.
> Look at the river – what have we here?
> Its currents flow with wine and beer,
> Claret and fine muscatel,
> Sherry one can drink as well.
> For a pittance all may drink these,
> New or old wine, sure to please.[40]

This medieval longing was rehearsed in folk traditions such as *The Feast of Fools*, where the peasant villagers sought to tip up existing society for the day, appointing a Lord of Misrule who would be led into the church sitting backward on a donkey, to then hold a mock sermon while the congregation brayed at the most serious parts, accompanied by priests dressed in women's clothes. Later on in England this rebel attitude would resurface in the subversive legend of Robin Hood.

Next came *Utopia* itself. The author, Sir Thomas More, is a complex historical figure – a forward thinking yet austere religious figure who becomes part of the elite, wields great power, and then crosses the interests of Henry VIII and is executed. But More also somehow embodies the tensions of straddling a fault-line of history — between the Middle Ages of the land of Cockaigne and the development of elements of early capitalism, with its brutal clearing of the land and the enclosures. More was a 'humanist' connected with like-minded thinkers on the continent, most important of who was Erasmus, part of a grouping that wanted rational thinking applied to the 'problems' that they saw developing in their societies.

Utopia was published in 1516 after a journey by More to visit his continental co-thinkers, and theorises about a reorganisation of society on lines of equality. The result is a strictly controlled, rather monkish society (not surprising given More's intense religiosity), but where everything produced is put into a common pot for the common good. This utopia is a six-hour day and a rudimentary democracy where people who run for office for personal gain are banned for life.

More is determinedly ambiguous about whether this new society should come about. His *Utopia* is essentially an inspired and prescient warning about what he saw as the dangers inherent on the one hand in the excesses of the new merchant class, with its drive to increase production of goods such as textiles, and its thirst to open up new markets overseas, and on the other hand the instability, disruption, disorientation and discontent this new force created. Some who have written on More have tried to wrench him out of his time and place and paint him as a proto-communist, but Morris took a more measured view:

> Doubtless the *Utopia* is a necessary part of a socialist's library; yet it seems to me that its value as a book for the study of sociology is rather historic than prophetic, and that we socialists should look upon it as a link between the surviving communism of the Middle Ages (becoming hopeless in More's time, and doomed to be soon wholly effaced by the advancing wave of commercial bureaucracy), and the hopeful and practical progressive movement of today. In fact I think More must be looked upon rather as the last of the old than the first of the new.

Apart from what was yet alive in him of medieval communist tradition, the spirit of association, which amongst other things produced the guilds, and which was strong in the medieval Catholic church itself, other influences were at work to make him take up his parable against the new spirit of his age. The action of the period of transition from medieval to commercial society with all its brutalities, was before his eyes; and though he was not alone in his time in condemning the injustice and cruelty of the revolution which destroyed the peasant life of England, and turned it into a grazing farm for the moneyed gentry; creating withal at one stroke the propertyless wage-earner, and the master-less vagrant ('pauper'), yet he saw deeper into its root-causes than any other man of his own day.[41]

After More we have a number of writings that have utopian elements thrown up during the turbulent rise and early expansion of British mercantile capitalism — from Shakespeare's *The Tempest* (1611), Milton's *Paradise Lost* (1662), to Swift's *Gulliver's Travels* (1727) and even Daniel Defoe's *Robinson Crusoe* (1719). Written from different class and social perspectives, they each deliver their own political, moral and religious lessons to their readers.

During the English Revolution there is an actual attempt to put utopia into action with the True Levellers, or 'Diggers', colonies on common land, most famously at St George's Hill, Surrey, founded by Gerrard Winstanley in April 1649. We do not return to utopia proper until the end of the 18th century. The catalyst is the French Revolution (1789-1815) – where the struggle for a new society beyond capitalism breaks out into the open. This reveals a myriad of human possibilities, which in their turn erupt in south London in the poetry of the magnificent visionary William Blake.

In Blake's Albion:

> The fields from Islington to Marylebone
> To Primrose Hill and Saint John's Wood,
> Were builded over with pillars of gold,
> And there Jerusalem's pillars stood.

In this world England and Albion occupy the same space — it is as though England is pregnant with the possibility of Albion. No longer is Utopia west of Spain, No Place, the Bahamas of *The Tempest* or Defoe's desert island. It is here: a transformation of present society. This is the massive leap forward, the imaginative product of the new revolutionary turmoil. During this period we witness the rise of the Utopian Socialists in the political and social arena—from St Simon and Fourier on the European continent to Robert Owen (whom Morris much admired) and his experiments in communist living in his factories in New Lanarkshire. In 1821 a group of radical printers did actually set up a commune of 21 families in Blake's Islington/Albion, at Spa Fields (today to be found tucked behind Exmouth Market).

This is the rich historic and literary lineage of Morris's *News from Nowhere*.

The narrative of Morris's story follows the same time-travel structure as Bellamy's *Looking Backwards*. But there is one difference – the nature of the transition to the new world. In an early chapter an old man named Hammond is asked to recall how the change came:

> 'Tell me one thing, if you can,' said I. 'Did the change, the 'revolution' it used to be called, come peacefully?'
>
> 'Peacefully?' said he; 'What peace was there amongst those poor confused wretches of the 19th century? It was war from beginning to end: bitter war, till hope and pleasure put an end to it'. [42]

Again in the chapter 'How the Change Came' Morris has Old Hammond tell the story of the insurrection that ushers in the decisive struggle. It starts with a massacre of workers during a demonstration in Trafalgar Square (the book having been written three years after Bloody Sunday) and although the revolution is set in 1952 the events and the characters (including Gladstone) place *News from Nowhere* in Victorian times.

Morris wants us to be sure that this future is not simply a dream, but a possibility growing out of the conditions of present society. So it would be wrong to brand *News from Nowhere* as merely a pleasant fantasy or a whimsical escape. Morris wants to engage the Victorian reader in the society he or she lives in — this is not fantastical, Morris is arguing that this is possible — it is what might be.

The detailed description of the events surrounding the revolution in *News from Nowhere* follows the only historical model that Morris knew — that of the bourgeois revolutions — but with the working class at the centre of affairs. The battle is fought out on the streets over a prolonged period before the revolution triumphs. But whatever model Morris based the revolution on, there can be no doubt that it is a refutation of gradualism. It is an advocacy of revolution and revolutionary change.

Morris also hints at the need for some kind of decisive organisation: 'But now the time called for immediate action, came forward the men capable of setting it on foot; and a vast network of workmen's associations grew up very speedily, whose avowed single object was the tiding over of the ship of state into a simple condition of communism'.[43]

He also describes how under communism people, their lives, their outlook on life and their relations with one another would be transformed. This is in contrast to Bellamy who thought the highpoint of people's leisure under communism would consist of listening to the radio!

Morris uses all his imaginative skills to create this new world, to draw the reader into it, as a means to convince them to become a socialist. He wanted the book to 'add a little hope to the struggle'. He called it the 'instinctive vision' of socialists, to be able to keep hold of the future goal at the centre of the everyday fight against the system. That people's interest in *News from Nowhere* has endured way beyond Morris's life is an indication that he was at least successful in this respect.

News from Nowhere also explored ecological issues. This is significant. Socialists have often been criticised for adhering to a system of thought that has nothing to say about the environment, and indeed is founded on the notion that humanity's needs are dependent upon the continued expansion of industrial development and so necessarily come above ecological considerations. However, this view is being increasingly challenged, for example by John Bellamy Foster (no relation to the author of *Looking Backwards*) in his book *Marx's Ecology – Materialism and Nature*.[44]

Foster argues that 'although there is a long history of denouncing Marx for a lack of ecological concern, it is now abundantly clear, after decades of debate, that this view does not at all fit with the evidence. On the contrary, as the Italian geographer Massimo Quaini has observed, 'Marx...denounced the spoliation of nature before a modern bourgeois ecological conscience was born'. From the start, Marx's notion of the alienation of human labor was connected to an understanding of the alienation of human beings from nature'.[45] Foster points out that 'the close connection between Marx's vision of communism and ecological sustainability is evident in the utopian conceptions of the acclaimed 19th century English artist, mastercraftsperson, designer, poet, and socialist activist William Morris…who was not only a firm advocate of Marxian socialism but also one of the formative Green thinkers in the English context'.[46]

Foster singles out *News from Nowhere* as an exposition of how a socialist society would reverse human beings' 'alienation from the earth: the ultimate foundation/ precondition for capitalism'. Foster finds that in *News from Nowhere* Morris writes 'in the spirit of Marx'. He cites the passage in *News from Nowhere* where Hammond explains that after the revolution those who previously packed out the conurbations 'flocked into the country villages, and so to say, flung themselves upon the freed land like a wild beast upon his prey'. However, Morris then says that after a while 'the invaders' 'yielded to the influence of their surroundings'. Morris sketches out how the division between town and country 'grew less and less' and in this he echoed Marx's conviction that there would in a world free of capitalist alienation be a 'restoration' of 'the metabolic relation between human beings and the earth'.

Morris was thus directly echoing Marx when he had Hammond explain the cycle of change:

> This is how we stand. England was once a country of clearings amongst the woods and wastes, with a few towns interspersed, which were fortresses for the feudal army, markets for the folk, gathering places for the craftsmen.

It then became a country of huge and foul smelling workshops and fouler gambling-dens, surrounded by an ill-kept, poverty-stricken farm, pillaged by the masters of the workshops. It is now a garden, where nothing is wasted and nothing is spoilt.[47]

*M*orris's vision of a broken and polluted landscape was not his alone. This growing environmental nightmare had previously been conjured up in 1845 by the then 24 year old Frederick Engels in the superb reportage that is his book *The Condition of the Working Class in England*. Here Engels describes a district of Manchester close by the latter day site of Manchester University:

The most horrible spot...is known as Little Ireland. In a rather deep hole, in a curve of the Medlock and surrounded on all four sides by tall factories and high embankments, covered with buildings, stand two groups of about 200 cottages, built chiefly back to back, in which live about 4,000 human beings, most of them Irish. The cottages are old, dirty, and of the smallest sort, the streets uneven, fallen into ruts and in part without drains or pavements; masses of refuse, offal, and sickening filth lie among standing pools in all directions; the atmosphere is poisoned by the effluvia from these; and laden and darkened by the smoke of a dozen tall factory chimneys.[48]

For the contemporary reader, Morris's writings do not only speak to 19th century industrial Britain. They encapsulate the despoliation of the environment that is accompanying modern globalisation in the global south. Witness this contemporary description of the southern Malaysian town

of Johor Baru:
> Through the heart of this sore afflicted town flows the Sungei Seggat, a river by only the most extravagant leap of the imagination. To say it 'flows' is to do hideous injustice to the word; the Sungei Seggat is a rank, black, stagnant, noisome ditch, filling the town centre of Johor Baru with the aroma of raw sewage and rotting carcasses. At the first sight and smell of the Sungei Seggat, it is no longer difficult to imagine the river that must flow through hell.[49]

The 'practical' Morris during the mid to late 1880s fully engaged his energies in the tasks of revolutionary socialism, replacing to a large extent his work at The Firm. He was utterly dedicated to the Socialist League and wanted to see it grow into an effective organisation: 'What I should like to have now, far more than anything else, would be a body of able, high-minded, competent men, who should act as instructors of the masses and as their leaders during critical periods of the movement. It goes without saying that a great proportion of these instructors and organisers should be working men... I should like to see 2,000 men of that stamp engaged in explaining the principles of rational, scientific socialism all over the kingdom'.[50]

To that end Morris tramped 'the kingdom' helping to set up branches. In its first year the League grew (from a handful) to maybe 600 members, with around 23 local branches from Dublin to Leeds, Birmingham, Norwich, many in London and outlying towns such as Croydon. More branches continued to be founded in towns such as Ipswich and Lancaster. Norwich was one of the most successful branches. As E P Thompson describes it, 'The Norwich Leaguers drove hard for working class support and headed the unemployed agitation. By Easter 1886, the branch was drawing audiences of 1,000 to its open-air meetings in the Market Place. From this time onwards, for the next 12 months, its membership rose rapidly'.[51] In contrast, the Edinburgh branch was kicked off in early 1885 with a 500 strong meeting, but had dwindled to five or six by the end of December. But by the 1887 annual conference the League could count maybe 1,000 members. On the horizon there were significant developments in the working class struggle of which the Socialist League should have been poised to take advantage.

A new fighting spirit and political awareness were growing and generalising among the working classes for the first time since the Chartists. The task that presented itself to revolutionaries was to influence these mass movements in the direction of revolutionary socialism. This is what Eleanor Marx and her partner Edward Aveling embarked on when they travelled to America in 1886 on a Marxist lecture tour in the midst of mass agitation over the establishment of an eight-hour day that included strikes and huge May Day demonstrations across the US.[52]

When the two Socialist League members returned to Britain they were invited by the East London Radical Clubs to lecture on 'The Working Classes of America'. It was the beginning of their agitational work in which they sought to reach the hitherto unorganised workers of the East End of London. It was the correct strategy that was to reap impressive and telling rewards.

The demand for an independent political voice for the working class was also beginning to be articulated in Britain. Partly this was to do with the discredited position of Gladstone and the Liberal Party among the most class conscious workers. Partly it was to do with experiments in workers' organisation abroad and partly it was to do with the presence of Irish Nationalist MPs in the British parliament. In the 1885 elections Irish Nationalist MPs returned to Westminster in greater numbers and wielded their votes in a disciplined manner, thus increasing the argument for a working class party that could contest elections. The big question, in Britain as elsewhere, was what kind of party that would be and whether it would carry Marxist politics. But for socialists to influence that outcome it was obvious they would have to take part in the debate in the first place.

Engels could feel that the working class was beginning to move. Over Easter 1887 a huge rally in Hyde Park against coercion in Ireland was big enough to encompass 15 speakers' platforms. Engels went straight to the point: 'It is now an immediate question of organising an English working men's party with an independent class programme. If it is successful, it will relegate to a back seat both the SDF and the Socialist League and that would be the most satisfactory end to the present squabbles'.[53] What had happened to the Socialist League that Engels himself had helped conceive for him to make such a damning judgement?

In truth the Socialist League was never the success that Morris and his fellow party members had wished it to be when they broke from the SDF. When the League had split from Hyndman it had carried two groupings with differing positions which were never resolved. Morris, unfortunately, thought at first that he could get away with balancing between the two. On the one hand, there were those, including Eleanor Marx and Edward Aveling in the League's Bloomsbury branch, who knew that the party had to connect with the day to day struggles of workers to grow or, as Engels put it, 'to fasten on the real needs of the people'. This included work in the trade unions; the kind of work Eleanor was doing in the East End, and taking part in the debate over parliamentary representation.

On the other hand, there was an anti-parliamentary grouping led by Joseph Lane. He was part of a triumvirate among the leadership who basically espoused an abstract position of non-engagement with workers apart from on an educational level. They condemned interventions in elections and the trade union struggle for the eight hour day which was taking place as mere 'palliatives'.

Unfortunately Morris' came down on the side of the latter due to his hostility to any discussion of the parliamentary question. (It was not until the 1890s that he was to alter his view.) He regarded any intervention in parliamentary politics as futile and positively harmful. No doubt the memory was still sharp as to his own painful introduction to parliamentary politics around the Eastern Question and the betrayals of Gladstone. So the self-isolating position adopted by the League in the 1885 election and thereafter was, 'Do not vote at all':

> When those who govern you see the number of votes cast at each election growing less and less, and note at the same time the growth of socialist bodies...terror fills their

souls, and they must...either use violence against you, which you will learn how to repel, or quail before you and sit helpless...until the time will come when you...will step in and claim your place, and become the new-born society of the world.[54]

As E P Thompson points out, it was no wonder those who left the SDF in disgust at Hyndman's intrigues did not go over to the League. The League, by their disdainful attitude to the question of elections, placed themselves outside the debate going on in the most class conscious elements in the working class movement that they needed to influence. As Engels rightly noted in 1886, 'You will not bring the numerous working class as a whole into the movement by sermons.' But that is precisely what Morris continued to do. In May 1886, at the same time as Eleanor Marx and Edward Aveling were in America, Morris declared:

> The *Commonweal*, then, will steadily continue to put forward the principles of international revolutionary socialism; will deprecate all meddling with parliamentary methods of 'reform'. Constitutionalism means the continuance of the present system; how can socialists, therefore, who aim at abolishing the system, support its support? [55]

This sectarian attitude was partly fuelled, certainly in the first half of the 1880s, by Morris's belief that the revolution was within reach. The job of socialists was therefore to propagandise for it. In 1884 he wrote, 'The hope of the speedy advent of [that] revolution is now being instilled into the thousands by the action of the Democratic Federation, and socialism is rapidly becoming something more in this country than a speculative philosophy'.[56]

But by 1887 Morris was forced to reassess his perspective. In February of that year he wrote a perspectives article entitled 'Facing the Worst of It'. Its timing was revealing. In distinctly measured prose for Morris, he warned the members of the League against attempting to 'prophesy as to the date of the realisation of our hopes'. He warned that any economic recovery would promote 'I told you so' declarations from capitalists as to the health of their system. Ironically he predicts that the period will be one of rising trade union militancy, which he sees it as the business of socialists to 'stimulate and support'. But he then moves quickly on to the certainty that a slump will follow. This was to be the period of politicisation of the working class. They would be propelled towards revolutionary conclusions. His overall message is that socialists should sit tight and do what they can in the meantime.[57]

This analysis sprang from his determinist views on the economy. Crudely, he held the belief that the more workers suffered under capitalism, the more they would be automatically driven to revolution. So when during 1886 British capitalism experienced a slight recovery, Morris's logic led him to hope that the situation would get worse. He wrote:

> Non-socialists will doubtless look on socialists who dread this recovery of trade as likely to calm down the present agitation as very dreadful persons... It is clear that this attempt at diverting the aspirations of the workers into the channel of mere self-interest has not the same chance of success when times are bad and trade slack.[58]

The operational outcome was that the Socialist League put

forward the purist slogan of 'Union among all workers', calling at all times for a 'general strike for socialism'. This in no way connected with the consciousness of a working class beginning to recover from a period of low struggle. The opportunities missed can only be guessed at. However, there were signs of the potential there was to intervene and lead disputes for those looking for them. As Thompson writes:

> Already in 1887 sections of workers were showing marked signs of sympathy with the socialists. In February 1887 (the same month as 'Facing the Worst of It' was written) when the Glasgow branch (of the League) called a demonstration...in support of striking Lanarkshire miners, over 20,000 attended: the miners' leaders spoke from the same platform as the leaguers.[59]

The truth was that, despite breaking from Hyndman at an organisational level, Morris still carried some of his politics, and saw trade unions with some suspicion and work among them as something which should be confined to socialist education. It should be noted that Morris's position was not uncommon on the left of the day but all the same it was to have grave consequences for the League. Where the Socialist League did intervene in industrial struggles, such as the Northumberland miners' strike in 1887, Morris was disappointed that the strikers did not automatically embrace revolutionary ideas en masse. He reports meetings where he received a great reception, and where the evening was inevitably rounded off by unanimous passing of a resolution in favour of proletarian revolution. Local comrades would then complain that later they could not raise those same workers out of what they considered passivity.[60]

Morris was also affected by the Bloody Sunday confrontation. His idea that the simple strength of the masses on the streets would be the mechanism that ushered in socialism was shattered in the face of police brutality. As he recalled in a telling phrase:

> I shall never forget how quickly these unarmed crowds were dispersed into clouds of dust. I found myself suddenly alone.[61]

However, the rout in Trafalgar Square was not the determining factor — there is no evidence that Morris's socialist campaigning slowed down significantly after Bloody Sunday. It was the League's inability to orientate itself on the working class that fatally weakened the organisation and demoralised Morris. It was not until March 1890 that Morris, looking back, saw what a dreadful mistake he had made at the time:

> Socialism is spreading, I suppose on the only lines it could spread, and the League is moribund simply because we are outside those lines, as I for one must always be... The main cause of the failure (which was obvious at least two years ago) is that you cannot keep a body together without giving it something to do in the present.[62]

Of course, it was not the case that all Socialist League members had Morris's attitude to the everyday struggles of workers, but from reading Morris's writings nowhere does one get the idea that these merited serious consideration for him or most other members of the leadership. The practical upshot was that both the Socialist League and the SDF were ill placed to take advantage of the upsurge of workers' struggles that heralded the New Unionism, ironically with the working class leaders emerging that Morris had hoped for from the start.

An inkling of what was possible was shown by the Leeds Socialist League branch. (It is important to note that the League branches outside London had more success due to them being outside the immediate influence of the leadership and therefore liable to take local initiatives outside party discipline.) At the centre of the Leeds branch was Tom Maguire, who had joined the Democratic Federation in his teens. By 1886 the dynamic Maguire and 20 or so comrades made an impression well above and beyond their numbers, due to their high level of activity. In 1889 the members had grown to 30. By the early summer of that year they were beginning to draw large crowds, up to 1,000 strong, to their open-air meetings. E P Thompson takes up the story:

> Then, at the beginning of July, some builders' labourers, who were at the meeting, began to discuss their grievances. Like the London dockers, they were paid at a rate of 5d an hour. Comrades Sweeny and Paylor... took the matter up and urged the men to form a union. The next Sunday, 30 July 30th, 3,000 labourers came to the sprouting place: Maguire, Paylor, Hill and Sweeney addressed them: 200 names were handed in; in the afternoon the Socialist League clubroom was crowded out; a provisional committee was elected; it decided at once to strike for 1/2d an hour; a general meeting was held, and the proposal was agreed to unanimously.[63]

Using the League club as a campaign centre, the building workers battled successfully with the contractors for a wage rise. Maguire remained a general helper and adviser to the new union that he had helped create. As Thompson says,

'The Leeds socialists had been transformed from being a curious sect into being the advisers and leaders of the unskilled workers of Leeds'.[64]

But in London, where the Socialist League leadership dominated, the story was very different, even though the same explosion of workers' struggle was manifesting itself. Low paid and generally unskilled workers, living in poverty and in fear of unemployment, working long hours with few rights and shut out of the exclusive New Model Unions, denied political representation and politicised by struggles such as Bloody Sunday, burst onto the political scene.

The historic strikes that followed were led by socialists. In July 1888 a strike by 700 terribly exploited Bryant & May match girls, their misery sensationally exposed in newspaper articles by Annie Besant (who had been in the National Secular Society with Edward Aveling), electrified the movement. Morris supported the strike, but with an aloofness that betrayed his overall position towards the strikes that were erupting around his ears.

Eleanor Marx had had to work independently of the League, agitating among the unskilled workers of the East End. Alongside her, working among the Beckton gas workers was SDF member Will Thorne. They launched a union modelled somewhat on the American Knights of Labour that Eleanor had observed on her 1886 American tour. Eleanor became an officer of the union and other SDFers like John Burns and Tom Mann, who had been agitating for an eight-hour day, took a lead in organising the gas workers. The union spread like wildfire and immediately won a bloodless victory, forcing their 12-hour day down to eight hours. This was followed in August 1889 by the London dock strike, which exploded from a small dispute into a stoppage by 60,000 men. Dockers' leader Ben Tillett turned to the socialists for help in the struggle for the docker's 'tanner' increase. Burns took the lead, organising daily demonstrations through the city.

The dockers' strike marked the rebirth of practical solidarity in the working class, with huge amounts of money raised, including a stunning £30,000 from Australian trade unionists. After five weeks the dockers won their 'tanner', providing inspiration for the whole working class and the foundation of new unions in many industries. That year there were over 1,200 stoppages and somewhere around 3.7 million working days taken in strike action. The previous year 509 strikes had been recorded.

Significantly the struggle had been led by revolutionary socialists, but largely outside the ranks of their organisations.

It was a tragedy, therefore, that in October 1889, in the afterglow of the dockers' victory and in the midst of the rebirth of the British working class, the Socialist League executive put out the following:

> In answer to numerous enquiries, the executive council... desires to express its opinion that members of the League do not in any way compromise their principles by taking part in strikes, but asks them not to let the revolutionary propaganda suffer thereby.[65]

Morris was not immune to the generalising effects the strikes were having. Writing admiringly of the dock workers, he could see that there was an 'element of conscious or semiconscious attack on the slave drivers generally...this is a revolt against oppression'.[64] But these insights did nothing to push Morris or the organisation into an active, leading, intervention in the disputes that were springing up. Such a position inevitably meant that Morris and the Socialist League saw an upsurge in workers' struggle completely pass them by. The League collapsed, and so did the fortunes of *Commonweal*. It was at this time that anarchists in London began to fight for control of the newspaper. Its circulation spiralled downwards as it became a platform for conspiratorial nonsense. For a time Morris continued to write a column, 'Notes on News', but in reality this was more out of loyalty to the paper than in agreement with the articles published alongside his. The Avelings' Bloomsbury branch left the League. Even Belfort Bax went back to the SDF.

The takeover of the League by the anarchists and Morris's willingness to try and keep *Commonweal* afloat have been used to insinuate that he 'went over' or was sympathetic to anarchism. This is not borne out in Morris's writing at the time. In fact in the pages of *Commonweal* he engaged in a polemic precisely against anarchism.[66]

As the Socialist League disintegrated Morris strove to keep his Hammersmith branch together. His energy was beginning to flag as he succumbed to ill health. Even though he was regarded as the elder statesman of the movement, he never stopped developing his politics. In fact, as E P Thompson successfully argues, Morris shifted on a whole number of issues away from the abstract position he had held earlier. In a sense he was going back to the unfulfilled 'stepping stones' that he had first encountered back in

1882, in which the fight for immediate gains was seen as important as long as the revolutionary aim was kept in view. In March 1893 he gave a lecture in Hammersmith called 'Communism'. In it he recognised that his belief in the 'inevitableness of a sudden a speedy change' had distorted the League's operation. Capitalist consolidation had not put paid to a future socialist society but it had ushered in the arrival of a 'businesslike administration' which it would take more than a street battle to topple.

He tempered his attitude towards reforms and elections, backing the struggle for a 'rise of wages, shortening of hours of labour, better education' and welcoming working class representation on bodies such as the London County Council.

At the same time his revolutionary light burned as bright as ever. Talking of the ultimate aim of reforms, he explained that there was no essential difference between socialism and communism: 'Communism is in fact the completion of socialism: when that ceases to be militant and becomes triumphant, it will be communism'.[67] In January, just in case anyone thought otherwise, he declared, 'I have not changed my mind about socialism.' In a gesture that demonstrated the centrality of revolutionary organisation in Morris's life, he made his peace with Hyndman and the SDF. The tragedy is that he was not well enough to explore the deepening understanding of Marxism he was developing.

Morris died on 3 October 1896 aged 63, almost his last words being, 'I want to get mumbo-jumbo out of the world.' The family doctor diagnosed that Morris had 'died a victim of his enthusiasm for spreading the principles of socialism'.

The newspapers moved between ignoring his socialism by talking about Morris the poet, and denouncing 'the force that drew him, without much regard for logic, or for the facts of life, into a sentimental socialism'.[68]

The socialist movement was in shock. Messages poured in from socialist organisations and individual workers alike: Robert Blatchford of the *Clarion* defended the Marxist Morris from all comers when he wrote:

> I cannot help thinking that it does not matter what goes into the *Clarion* this week, because William Morris is dead...he was our best man, and he is dead. How can we think of the movement today but as a thing struck motionless? I have just been reading the obituary notices in some of the Labour papers, and I feel sick and sorry. The fine phrases, the elaborate compliments, the ostentatious parade of their own erudition, and the little covert sneers at the socialism Morris loved: all the tawdry upholsteries of these journalistic undertakers seems like desecration... Morris was not only a genius, he was a man. Strike at him where you would, he rang true.[69]

1. A L Morton, op cit, p86.
2. Ibid, p87.
3. Ibid, p89.
4. Ibid, p91.
5. Ibid, p91.
6. Ibid, p92.
7. Ibid, p93.
8. Ibid, p94.
9. Ibid, p95.
10. Nicholas Salmon, op cit, p612.
11. A L Morton, op cit, p106. As E P Thompson recounts: One is reminded of (George Bernard) Shaw's story of accompanying Morris through the Merton Abbey works. Directing attention to a dull and mechanical task he 'dared to say'; 'You should get a machine to do that.' 'I've ordered one', was Morris's reply. E P Thompson, op cit, p654.
12. E P Thompson, op cit, p654.
13. William Morris, *A Factory As It Might Be*, Mushroom, 1994, p9.
14. A L Morton, op cit, p129.
15. Nicholas Salmon, op cit, p397.
16. John Reed, 'The Origin of Workers' Control in Russia', in *Shaking The World: John Reed's Revolutionary Journalism*, edited by John Newsinger, Bookmarks London, 1998, p136.
17. Nicholas Salmon, op cit, p 87.
18. Arthur Ransom, *Six Weeks in Russia 1919*, Redwords 1992, p105-106.

19. Fiona MacCarthy, op cit, p599.

20. Letters to Thomas Armstrong, director of the arts division of the South Kensington Museum (now Victoria and Albert), 13 March 1893. In the *Collected Letters of William Morris,* edited by Norman Kelvin, Princetown 1996, Volume IV, 1893-1896, pp23-24. The carpet, said to be one of the largest ever produced is thought to have originated in Ardabil, Persia (now Iran), from the 16th century burial place of a ruler of the Muslim Safavid dynasty.

21. E P Thompson, op cit, p665.

22. Ibid, p444.

23. Ibid, p37.

24. *Three Works by William Morris*, edited by A L Morton, Lawrence and Wishart, 1986, p167.

25. Ibid p143.

26. R B Dobson, *The Peasants Revolt of 1381*, Pitman 1970, p273.

27. E P Thompson, op cit, p723.

28. *Three Works*, op cit, p53.

29. Ibid, p109.

30. Ibid, p67.

31. E P Thompson, op cit, p700.

32. A L Morton, *The English Utopia* (Lawrence and Wishart, 1978), p196.

33. Ibid, p197.

34. See Bellamy quoted in Morton and Tate, op cit, p196.

35. A L Morton, op cit p493.

36. Nicholas Salmon, op cit, p419.

37. Ibid, p421.

38. J W Mackail, quoted in A L Morton and George Tate, op cit, p208

39. See Herman Pleij, *Dreaming of Cockaigne: Medieval Fantasises of the Perfect Life,* trans Diane Webb, Columbia 2001, p210.

40. Ibid, p34

41. William Morris, Foreword to Thomas More's *Utopia*, www.marxists.org/archive/morris/works/1893/utopia

42. 'News From Nowhere' in *Three Works*, op cit, p287.

43. Ibid, p304.

44. John Bellamy Foster, *Marx's Ecology – Materialism and Nature*, Monthly Review Press, March 2000.

45. Ibid, p9.
46. Ibid, p176.
47. 'News From Nowhere' in *Three Works*, op cit, p254
48. Frederick Engels, *The Condition of the Working Class in England in 1844*, Oxford 1993, p72
49. Quoted in Victor Mallet, *The Trouble With Tigers: The Rise and Fall of South East Asia,* HarperCollins Business 2000, p168.
50. E P Thompson, op cit, p379.
51. Ibid, p418.
52. Yvonne Kapp, op cit, p148.
53. Engels quoted in Morton & Tate, op cit, p178.
54. E P Thompson, op cit, p405.
55. Nicholas Salmon, op cit, p135.
56. Ibid, p55.
57. Ibid, p222.
58. Ibid, pp207-208.
59. E P Thompson, op cit, p437.
60. Ibid, p438.
61. Ibid, p490.
62. Yvonne Kapp, op cit, pp366-7.
63. E P Thompson, op cit, p528.
64. Ibid, p529.
65. Ibid, p531.
66. Nicholas Salmon, op cit, p453.
67. Ibid, p415.
68. Fiona MacCarthy, op cit, p672.
69. E P Thompson, op cit, p638.

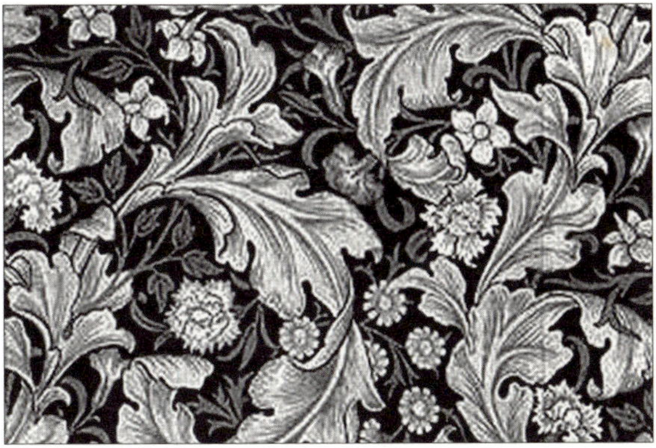

Bibliography & further reading

WILLIAM MORRIS WRITINGS

Three Works By William Morris: a Dream of John Ball, the Pilgrims of Hope, News From Nowhere, introduction by A L Morton (Lawrence & Wishart 1986)
William Morris on Art and Socialism, introduction by Norman Kelvin (Dover Publications 2003)
William Morris: Political Writings Contributions to Justice and Commonweal 1883-1890, edited by Nicholas Salmon (Thoemmes Press 1994)
Political Writings of William Morris, introduction and edited by A L Morton (Lawrence & Wishart 1984)
William Morris by himself: Designs and writings, edited by Gillian Naylor (Time Warner 2004)
The Relations of Art to Labour (William Morris Society 2004)
Our Country Right or Wrong, a critical edition edited by Florence Boos (William Morris Society 2008)
Useful Work Versus Useless Toil, (Penguin Classics, 2008)

On William Morris

Peter Faulkner, *Against the Age: an introduction to William Morris* (George, Allan & Unwin 1980)
William Morris Today, exhibition catalogue ICA 1984.
Ruth Kinna, *William Morris: The Art of Socialism* (University of Wales Press 2000)
Fiona McCarthy, *William Morris: A Life for Our Time* (Faber & Faber 1994)
Tony Pinkney, *William Morris in Oxford* (Illuminati 2007)
E P Thompson *William Morris, from Romantic to Revolutionary* (Merlin Press 2011)
Paul Thompson, *The Work of William Morris* (Oxford University Press 1993)
Ray Watkinson, *William Morris as Designer* (Trefoil 1979)

General History

John Charlton, *The Chartists: The First National Workers Movement* (Pluto Press 1997)
John Charlton, *'It just went like tinder': The mass movement & New Unionism in Britiain 1889* (Redwords 1999)
Frederick Engels, *The Condition of the Working Class in England in 1844* (Dodo Press 2007)
Yvonne Kapp, *Eleanor Marx Volumes 1 & 2*, (Virargo 1979)
A L Morton & George Tate, *The British Labour Movement 1770 - 1920* (Lawrence & Wishart 1980)
John Saville, *The Consolidation of the Capitalist State* (Pluto Press 1994)

OTHER BOOKS OF INTEREST

John Bellamy Foster, *Marx's Ecology – materialism and nature* (Monthly Review Press 2000)
A L Morton, *The English Utopia* (Lawrence & Wishart 1969)
Herman Pleij, *Dreaming of Cockaigne: Medieval Fantasies of the Perfect Life*, translated by Diane Webb (Columbia 2001)

WILLIAM MORRIS ASSOCIATED WEBSITES

The William Morris Internet Archive
http://www.marxists.org/archive/morris/works/index.htm

William Morris Society
http://www.morrissociety.org/

William Morris Gallery, Walthamstow
http://www.walthamforest.gov.uk/william-morris

*William Morris speaking from the
Socialist League wagon, May Day 1883*

CHANTS FOR SOCIALISTS
William Morris

downloaded from
www.marxists.org/archive/morris/works/1894/chants

1. the day is coming

Come hither, lads, and hearken, for a tale there is to tell,
Of the wonderful days a-coming, when all shall be better than well.
And the tale shall be told of a country, a land in the midst of the sea,
And folk shall call it England in the days that are going to be.

There more than one in a thousand in the days that are yet to come
Shall have some hope of the morrow, some joy of the ancient home.
For then — laugh not, but listen to this strange tale of mine —
All folk that are in England shall be better lodged than swine.

Then a man shall work and bethink him, and rejoice in the deeds of his hand,
Nor yet come home in the even too faint and weary to stand.
Men in that time a-coming shall work and have no fear
For to-morrow's lack of earning and the hunger-wolf anear.

I tell you this for a wonder, that no man then shall be glad
Of his fellow's fall and mishap to snatch at the work he had.
For that which the worker winneth shall then be his indeed,
Nor shall half be reaped for nothing by him that sowed no seed.

O strange new wonderful justice! But for whom shall we gather the gain?
For ourselves and for each of our fellows, and no hand shall labour in vain.
Then all Mine and all Thine shall be Ours, and no more shall any man crave
For riches that serve for nothing but to fetter a friend for a slave.

And what wealth then shall be left us when none shall gather gold
To buy his friend in the market, and pinch and pine the sold?
Nay, what save the lovely city, and the little house on the hill,
And the wastes and the woodland beauty, and the happy fields we till;

And the homes of ancient stories, the tombs of the mighty dead;
And the wise men seeking out marvels, and the poet's teeming head;
And the painter's hand of wonder; and the marvellous fiddle-bow,
And the banded choirs of music: all those that do and know.

For all these shall be ours and all men's, nor shall any lack a share
Of the toil and the gain of living in the days when the world grows fair.
Ah! such are the days that shall be! But what are the deeds of to-day,
In the days of the years we dwell in, that wear our lives away?

Why, then, and for what are we waiting? There are three words to speak:
WE WILL IT, and what is the foeman but the dream-strong wakened and weak?
O why and for what are we waiting? While our brothers droop and die,
And on every wind of the heavens a wasted life goes by.

How long shall they reproach us where crowd on crowd they dwell,
Poor ghosts of the wicked city, the gold-crushed hungry hell?
Through squalid life they laboured, in sordid grief they died,
Those sons of a mighty mother, those props of England's pride.

They are gone; there is none can undo it, nor save our souls from the curse;
But many a million cometh, and shall they be better or worse?
It is we must answer and hasten, and open wide the door
For the rich man's hurrying terror, and the slow-foot hope of the poor.

Yea, the voiceless wrath of the wretched, and their unlearned discontent,
We must give it voice and wisdom till the waiting-tide be spent.
Come, then, since all things call us, the living and the dead,
And o'er the weltering tangle a glimmering light is shed.

Come, then, let us cast off fooling, and put by ease and rest,
For the CAUSE alone is worthy till the good days bring the best.
Come, join in the only battle wherein no man can fail,
Where whoso fadeth and dieth, yet his deed shall still prevail.

Ah! come, cast off all fooling, for this, at least, we know:
That the Dawn and the Day is coming, and forth the Banners go.

2. the voice of toil

I heard men saying, Leave hope and praying,
All days shall be as all have been;
To-day and to-morrow bring fear and sorrow,
The never-ending toil between.

When Earth was younger mid toil and hunger,
In hope we strove, and our hands were strong;
Then great men led us, with words they fed us,
And bade us right the earthly wrong.

Go read in story their deeds and glory,
Their names amidst the nameless dead;
Turn then from lying to us slow-dying
In that good world to which they led;

Where fast and faster our iron master,
The thing we made, for ever drives,
Bids us grind treasure and fashion pleasure
For other hopes and other lives.

Where home is a hovel and dull we grovel,
Forgetting that the world is fair;
Where no babe we cherish, lest its very soul perish;
Where our mirth is crime, our love a snare.

Who now shall lead us, what god shall heed us
As we lie in the hell our hands have won?
For us are no rulers but fools and befoolers,
The great are fallen, the wise men gone.

I heard men saying, Leave tears and praying,
The sharp knife heedeth not the sheep;
Are we not stronger than the rich and the wronger,
When day breaks over dreams and sleep?

Come, shoulder to shoulder ere the world grows older!
Help lies in nought but thee and me;
Hope is before us, the long years that bore us
Bore leaders more than men may be.

Let dead hearts tarry and trade and marry,
And trembling nurse their dreams of mirth,
While we the living our lives are giving
To bring the bright new world to birth.

Come, shoulder to shoulder ere earth grows older
The Cause spreads over land and sea;
Now the world shaketh, and fear awaketh
And joy at last for thee and me.

3. no master

Saith man to man, We've heard and known
That we no master need
To live upon this earth, our own,
In fair and manly deed.
The grief of slaves long passed away
For us hath forged the chain,
Till now each worker's patient day
Builds up the House of Pain.

And we, shall we too, crouch and quail,
Ashamed, afraid of strife,
And lest our lives untimely fail
Embrace the Death in Life?
Nay, cry aloud, and have no fear,
We few against the world;
Awake, arise! the hope we bear
Against the curse is hurled.

It grows and grows--are we the same,
The feeble band, the few?
Or what are these with eyes aflame,
And hands to deal and do?
This is the host that bears the word,
No MASTER HIGH OR LOW —
A lightning flame, a shearing sword,
A storm to overthrow.

4. all for the cause

Hear a word, a word in season, for the day is drawing nigh,
When the Cause shall call upon us, some to live, and some to die!
He that dies shall not die lonely, many an one hath gone before;
He that lives shall bear no burden heavier than the life they bore.

Nothing ancient is their story, e'en but yesterday they bled,
Youngest they of earth's beloved, last of all the valiant dead.
E'en the tidings we are telling was the tale they had to tell,
E'en the hope that our hearts cherish, was the hope for which they fell.

In the grave where tyrants thrust them, lies their labour and their pain,
But undying from their sorrow springeth up the hope again.
Mourn not therefore, nor lament it, that the world outlives their life;
Voice and vision yet they give us, making strong our hands for strife.

Some had name, and fame, and honour, learn'd they were, and wise and strong;
Some were nameless, poor, unlettered, weak in all but grief and wrong.
Named and nameless all live in us; one and all they lead us yet
Every pain to count for nothing, every sorrow to forget.

Hearken how they cry, 'O happy, happy ye that ye were born
In the sad slow night's departing, in the rising of the morn.
'Fair the crown the Cause hath for you, well to die or well to live
Through the battle, through the tangle, peace to gain or peace to give.'

Ah, it may be! Oft meseemeth, in the days that yet shall be,
When no slave of gold abideth 'twixt the breadth of sea to sea,
Oft, when men and maids are merry, ere the sunlight leaves the earth,
And they bless the day beloved, all too short for all their mirth,

Some shall pause awhile and ponder on the bitter days of old,
Ere the toil of strife and battle overthrew the curse of gold;
Then 'twixt lips of loved and lover solemn thoughts of us shall rise;
We who once were fools and dreamers, then shall be the brave and wise.

There amidst the world new-builded shall our earthly deeds abide,
Though our names be all forgotten, and the tale of how we died.
Life or death then, who shall heed it, what we gain or what we lose?
Fair flies life amid the struggle, and the Cause for each shall choose.

Hear a word, a word in season, for the day is drawing nigh,
When the Cause shall call upon us, some to live, and some to die!

5. the march of the workers

What is this, the sound and rumour? What is this that all men hear,
Like the wind in hollow valleys when the storm is drawing near,
Like the rolling on of ocean in the eventide of fear?
'Tis the people marching on.

Whither go they, and whence come they? What are these of whom ye tell?
In what country are they dwelling 'twixt the gates of heaven and hell?
Are they mine or thine for money? Will they serve a master well?
Still the rumour's marching on.

Hark the rolling of the thunder!
Lo the sun! and lo thereunder
Riseth wrath, and hope, and wonder,
And the host comes marching on.

Forth they come from grief and torment; on they wend toward health and mirth,
All the wide world is their dwelling, every corner of the earth.
Buy them, sell them for thy service! Try the bargain what 'tis worth,
For the days are marching on.

These are they who build thy houses, weave thy raiment, win thy wheat,
Smooth the rugged, fill the barren, turn the bitter into sweet,
All for thee this day — and ever. What reward for them is meet
Till the host comes marching on?

Hark the rolling of the thunder!
Lo the sun! and lo thereunder
Riseth wrath, and hope, and wonder,
And the host comes marching on.

Many a hundred years passed over have they laboured deaf and blind;
Never tidings reached their sorrow, never hope their toil might find.
Now at last they've heard and hear it, and the cry comes down the wind,
And their feet are marching on.

O ye rich men hear and tremble! for with words the sound is rife:
'Once for you and death we laboured; changed henceforward is the strife.
We are men, and we shall battle for the world of men and life;
And our host is marching on.'

Hark the rolling of the thunder!
Lo the sun! and lo thereunder
Riseth wrath, and hope, and wonder,
And the host comes marching on.

'Is it war, then? Will ye perish as the dry wood in the fire?
Is it peace? Then be ye of us, let your hope be our desire.
Come and live! for life awaketh, and the world shall never tire;
And hope is marching on.

'On we march then, we the workers, and the rumour that ye hear
Is the blended sound of battle and deliv'rance drawing near;
For the hope of every creature is the banner that we bear,
And the world is marching on.'

Hark the rolling of the thunder!
Lo the sun! and lo thereunder
Riseth wrath, and hope, and wonder,
And the host comes marching on.

6. down among the dead men

Come, comrades, come, your glasses clink;
Up with your hands a health to drink,
The health of all that workers be,
In every land, on every sea.
And he that will this health deny,
Down among the dead men, down among the dead men,
Down, down, down, down,
Down among the dead men let him lie!

Well done! now drink another toast,
And pledge the gath'ring of the host,
The people armed in brain and hand,
To claim their rights in every land.
And he that will this health deny,
Down among the dead men, down among the dead men,
Down, down, down, down,
Down among the dead men let him lie!

There's liquor left; come, let's be kind,
And drink the rich a better mind,
That when we knock upon the door,
They may be off and say no more.
And he that will this health deny,
Down among the dead men, down among the dead men,
Down, down, down, down,
Down among the dead men let him lie!

Now, comrades, let the glass blush red,
Drink we the unforgotten dead
That did their deeds and went away,
Before the bright sun brought the day.
And he that will this health deny,
Down among the dead men, down among the dead men,
Down, down, down, down,
Down among the dead men let him lie!

The Day? Ah, friends, late grows the night;
Drink to the glimmering spark of light,
The herald of the joy to be,
The battle-torch of thee and me!
And he that will this health deny,
Down among the dead men, down among the dead men,
Down, down, down, down,
Down among the dead men let him lie!

Take yet another cup in hand
And drink in hope our little band;
Drink strife in hope while lasteth breath,
And brotherhood in life and death;
And he that will this health deny,
Down among the dead men, down among the dead men,
Down, down, down, down,
Down among the dead men let him lie!

7. *a death song**

What cometh here from west to east awending?
And who are these, the marchers stern and slow?
We bear the message that the rich are sending
Aback to those who bade them wake and know.
Not one, not one, nor thousands must they slay,
But one and all if they would dusk the day.

We asked them for a life of toilsome earning,
They bade us bide their leisure for our bread;
We craved to speak to tell our woeful learning:
We come back speechless, bearing back our dead.
Not one, not one, nor thousands must they slay,
But one and all if they would dusk the day.

They will not learn; they have no ears to hearken.
They turn their faces from the eyes of fate;
Their gay-lit halls shut out the skies that darken.
But, lo! this dead man knocking at the gate.
Not one, not one, nor thousands must they slay,
But one and all if they would dusk the day.

Here lies the sign that we shall break our prison;
Amidst the storm he won a prisoner's rest;
But in the cloudy dawn the sun arisen
Brings us our day of work to win the best.
Not one, not one, nor thousands must they slay,
But one and all if they would dusk the day.

Written for the funeral of Alfred Linnell — 18 December 1887

8. may day, 1892

The Workers
O Earth, once again cometh Spring to deliver
Thy winter-worn heart, O thou friend of the Sun;
Fair blossom the meadows from river to river
And the birds sing their triumph o'er winter undone.

O Earth, how a-toiling thou singest thy labour
And upholdest the flower-crowned cup of thy bliss,
As when in the feast-tide drinks neighbour to neighbour
And all words are gleeful, and nought is amiss.

But we, we, O Mother, through long generations,
We have toiled and been fruitful, but never with thee
Might we raise up our bowed heads and cry to the nations
To look on our beauty, and hearken our glee.

Unlovely of aspect, heart-sick and a-weary
On the season's fair pageant all dim-eyed we gaze;
Of thy fairness we fashion a prison-house dreary
And in sorrow wear over each day of our days.

The Earth
O children! O toilers, what foemen beleaguer
The House I have built you, the Home I have won?
Full great are my gifts, and my hands are all eager
To fill every heart with the deeds I have done.

The Workers
The foemen are born of thy body, O Mother,
In our shape are they shapen, their voice is the same;
And the thought of their hearts is as ours and no other;
It is they of our own house that bring us to shame.

The Earth
Are ye few? Are they many? What words have ye spoken
To bid your own brethren remember the Earth?
What deeds have ye done that the bonds should be broken,
And men dwell together in good-will and mirth?

The Workers
They are few, we are many: and yet, O our Mother,
Many years were we wordless and nought was our deed,
But now the word flitteth from brother to brother:
We have furrowed the acres and scattered the seed.

The Earth
Win on then unyielding, through fair and foul weather,
And pass not a day that your deed shall avail.
And in hope every spring-tide come gather together
That unto the Earth ye may tell all your tale.

Then this shall I promise, that I am abiding
The day of your triumph, the ending of gloom,
And no wealth that ye will then my hand shall be hiding
And the tears of the spring into roses shall bloom.

9. may day, 1894

Clad is the year in all her best,
The land is sweet and sheen;
Now Spring with Summer at her breast,
Goes down the meadows green.

Here are we met to welcome in
The young abounding year,
To praise what she would have us win
Ere winter draweth near.

For surely all is not in vain,
This gallant show she brings;
But seal of hope and sign of gain,
Beareth this Spring of springs.

No longer now the seasons wear
Dull, without any tale
Of how the chain the toilers bear
Is growing thin and frail.

But hope of plenty and goodwill
Flies forth from land to land,
Nor any now the voice can still
That crieth on the hand.
A little while shall Spring come back

And find the Ancient Home
Yet marred by foolish waste and lack,
And most enthralled by some.

A little while, and then at last
Shall the greetings of the year
Be blent with wonder of the past
And all the griefs that were.

A little while, and they that meet
The living year to praise,
Shall be to them as music sweet
That grief of bye-gone days.

So be we merry to our best,
Now the land is sweet and sheen,
And Spring with Summer at her breast
Goes down the meadows green.

10. the message of the March wind

Fair now is the springtide, now earth lies beholding
With the eyes of a lover the face of the sun;
Long lasteth the daylight, and hope is enfolding
The green-growing acres with increase begun.

Now sweet, sweet it is through the land to be straying
Mid the birds and the blossoms and the beasts of the field;
Love mingles with love, and no evil is weighing
On thy heart or mine, where all sorrow is healed.

From township to township, o'er down and by tillage
Far, far have we wandered and long was the day,
But now cometh eve at the end of the village,
Where over the grey wall the church riseth grey.

There is wind in the twilight; in the white road before us
The straw from the ox-yard is blowing about;
The moon's rim is rising, a star glitters o'er us,
And the vane on the spire-top is swinging in doubt.

Down there dips the highway, toward the bridge crossing over
The brook that runs on to the Thames and the sea.
Draw closer, my sweet, we are lover and lover;
This eve art thou given to gladness and me.

Shall we be glad always? Come closer and hearken:
Three fields further on, as they told me down there,
When the young moon has set, if the March sky should darken,
We might see from the hill-top the great city's glare.

Hark, the wind in the elm-boughs! From London it bloweth,
And telling of gold, and of hope and unrest;
Of power that helps not; of wisdom that knoweth,
But teacheth not aught of the worst and the best.

Of the rich men it telleth, and strange is the story
How they have, and they hanker, and grip far and wide;
And they live and they die, and the earth and its glory
Has been but a burden they scarce might abide.

Hark! the March wind again of a people is telling;
Of the life that they live there, so haggard and grim,
That if we and our love amidst them had been dwelling
My fondness had faltered, thy beauty grown dim.

This land we have loved in our love and our leisure
For them hangs in heaven, high out of their reach;
The wide hills o'er the sea-plain for them have no pleasure,
The grey homes of their fathers no story to teach.

The singers have sung and the builders have builded,
The painters have fashioned their tales of delight;
For what and for whom hath the world's book been gilded,
When all is for these but the blackness of night?

How long and for what is their patience abiding?
How oft and how oft shall their story be told,
While the hope that none seeketh in darkness is hiding
And in grief and in sorrow the world groweth old?

Come back to the inn, love, and the lights and the fire,
And the fiddler's old tune and the shuffling of feet;
For there in a while shall be rest and desire,
And there shall the morrow's uprising be sweet.

Yet, love, as we wend the wind bloweth behind us
And beareth the last tale it telleth to-night,
How here in the spring-tide the message shall find us;
For the hope that none seeketh is coming to light.

Like the seed of midwinter, unheeded, unperished,
Like the autumn-sown wheat 'neath the snow lying green,
Like the love that o'ertook us, unawares and uncherished,
Like the babe 'neath thy girdle that groweth unseen,

So the hope of the people now buddeth and groweth —
Rest fadeth before it, and blindness and fear;
It biddeth us learn all the wisdom it knoweth;
It hath found us and held us, and biddeth us hear:

For it beareth the message: 'Rise up on the morrow
And go on your ways toward the doubt and the strife;
Join hope to our hope and blend sorrow with sorrow,
And seek for men's love in the short days of life.'

But lo, the old inn, and the lights and the fire,
And the fiddler's old tune and the shuffling of feet;
Soon for us shall be quiet and rest and desire,
And to-morrow's uprising to deeds shall be sweet.

To find out more about William Morris and the Arts & Crafts movement visit:

■ *William Morris Gallery*
Lloyd Park, Forest Road, London E17 4PP
www.lbwf.gov.uk/wmg

■ *Kelmscott Manor*
Kelmscott, Lechlade, Glos GL7 3HJ
www.kelmscottmanor.co.uk

■ *Red House*
Red House Lane, Bexleyheath DA6 8JF
www.nationaltrust.org.uk

■ *Victoria and Albert Museum*
Cromwell Road, London SW7 2RL
www.vam.ac.uk

Join:
■ *William Morris Society*
www.morrissociety.org

Also available from Redwords

Poems of Protest by William Morris
With an introduction by Michael Rosen, £6.99

Though most know him for his design work, William Morris was also an accomplished writer whose poetry was used as songs and chants for the socialist movement. This volume includes work that has not been published since first appearing as propaganda in The Commonweal, *the paper of Morris's Socialist League. Michael Rosen argues that his socialist poetry was part of a long tradition of protest writing and a signpost for future struggles.*

Also included is How I Became a Socialist *by William Morris and an afterword* The Communist Poet-Laureate *by the Morris scholar Nicholas Salmon.*

www.redwords.org.uk
1 Bloomsbury Street, London WC1B 3QE

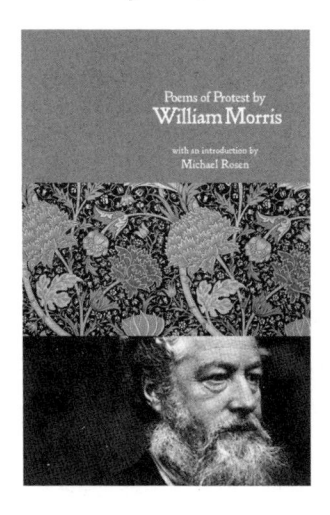

Also available from Bookmarks the **socialist bookshop**

The Point is to Change It!
An introduction to Marxist philosophy
by John Molyneux
£7

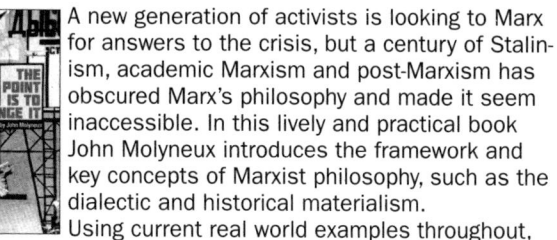

A new generation of activists is looking to Marx for answers to the crisis, but a century of Stalinism, academic Marxism and post-Marxism has obscured Marx's philosophy and made it seem inaccessible. In this lively and practical book John Molyneux introduces the framework and key concepts of Marxist philosophy, such as the dialectic and historical materialism.
Using current real world examples throughout, he illustrates the relevance of Marxism for trade unionists, activists and anyone who wants to change the world today.

Defending Multiculturalism: A Guide for the Movement
Edited by Hassan Mahamdallie
£8
This vibrant, hard-hitting and informative collection of essays sets out to defend Britain's multicultural way of life. The contributors challenge David Cameron and others' assertions that multiculturalism is to blame for dividing society.
Contributors include Peter Hain MP, Professor Tariq Modood, Liz Fekete, Professor Danny Dorling, Salma Yaqoob, Ken Livingstone, Edie Friedman, Sabby Dhalu, Martin Smith, Billy Hayes, Weyman Bennett and Dilowar Khan. Poetry by Michael Rosen, Zita Holbourne, Benjamin Zephaniah and Avaes Mohammed, photos by Rehan Jamil.

Bookmarks bookshop,
1 Bloomsbury Street, London WC1B 3QE
020 7637 1848 enquiries@bookmarks.uk.com

www.bookmarksbookshop.co.uk

bookmarks
the socialist bookshop